THE TEACHER AS A DECISION-MAKER

THE TEACHER AS A DECISION-MAKER

Dale L. Brubaker
The University of North Carolina

WM. C. BROWN COMPANY PUBLISHERS
Dubuque, Iowa

Library of Congress Catalog Card Number: 77–98544

ISBN 0–697–06014–4

Third Printing, 1972

Printed in the United States of America

To Ardis Snyder
For Making A Difference In
Her Students' Lives

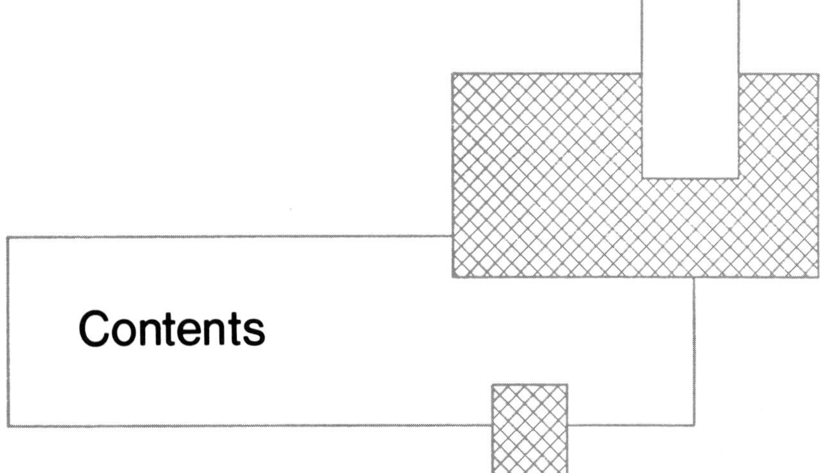

Contents

Case Studies

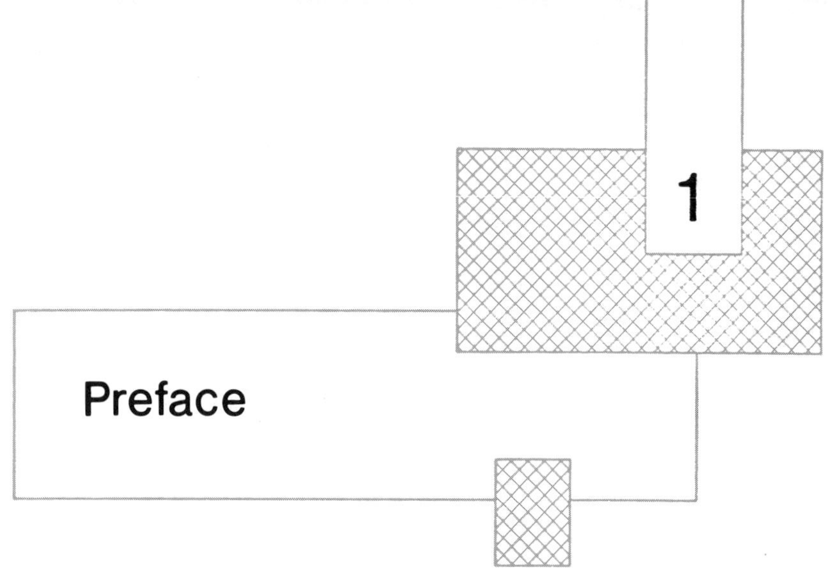

Preface

The advantages of the case study approach to decision-making are many: (1) the prospective teacher can empathize with those who have actually been confronted with teaching situations; (2) the prospective teacher can see that there is no "right" answer to any one teaching situation, thereby taking into account the many variables involved in being a teacher; and (3) dialogue as to how a teacher should handle a particular situation is stimulated in education courses and programs.

This book is designed for prospective teachers and in-service teachers in teacher education programs. It may serve as a text or supplement to a text.

Part I of the book has been written in order to give the reader the conceptual tools and framework in which to understand the school as a social system. The result should be to provide the reader with the analytical tools which will help him to understand any social system in our society.

Part II deals with the important matter of finding a teaching position. Although there is much verbal dialogue on this matter, there has been little writing done in this area. Chapters 3 through 7 begin with an introductory essay and are followed by case studies in which the reader is placed in the position of a teacher.

Part III focuses on the sources of conflict in the school as a social system. Conflict between teachers and parents, teachers and administrators, teachers and teachers, and teachers and students, is the subject of this section of the book.

Possible courses of action in resolving the problem situation created in each case study are included at the end of each chapter. The reader may decide whether or not he wishes to turn to the end of the chapter in order to weigh alternative responses. The responses are included because most prospective teachers have not had sufficient acquaintance with classrooms, in the capacity of teacher, to foresee the myriad of responses possible in dealing with the many problems facing the teacher. More than one response may be appropriate in resolving each case. A blank space is also provided following each list of responses in the event the reader decides that none of the responses is appropriate. It may be wise to consider whether it is more prudent at times to do nothing rather than attempt to solve the question in conflict.

Professor Carlton E. Beck was extremely helpful with his perceptive comments and suggestions as to how the manuscript might be improved. The author is most appreciative to him for his assistance. Mr. Dennis L. Sonnenburg was also very helpful in reviewing and revising the original manuscript. As a master teacher in the schools, he brought perception and realism to this manuscript.

I wish to thank the many teachers who provided case studies in interviews, both individual and group, and questionnaires. Their interest in this project was most heartening. Names of individuals and schools in the case studies have been changed so that any similarities to present school systems or individuals are incidental.

Appreciation is also due Prentice-Hall, Inc., for permission to use the conceptual model of the social system found in *Rural Sociology* by Charles P. Loomis and J. Allen Beegle.*

Finally, my sincere gratitude is expressed to Mrs. Cleo E. Dietz and Mrs. Dorothy Damewood, each of whom typed several drafts of this manuscript as well as others.

Dale L. Brubaker

Milwaukee, Wisconsin

*The author is indebted to Charles P. Loomis and J. Allan Beegle for the conceptual framework employed in Chapter One. See: Charles P. Loomis and J. Allan Beegle, *Rural Sociology*, Englewood Cliffs, N. J., Prentice-Hall, 1960. Chapter 1.

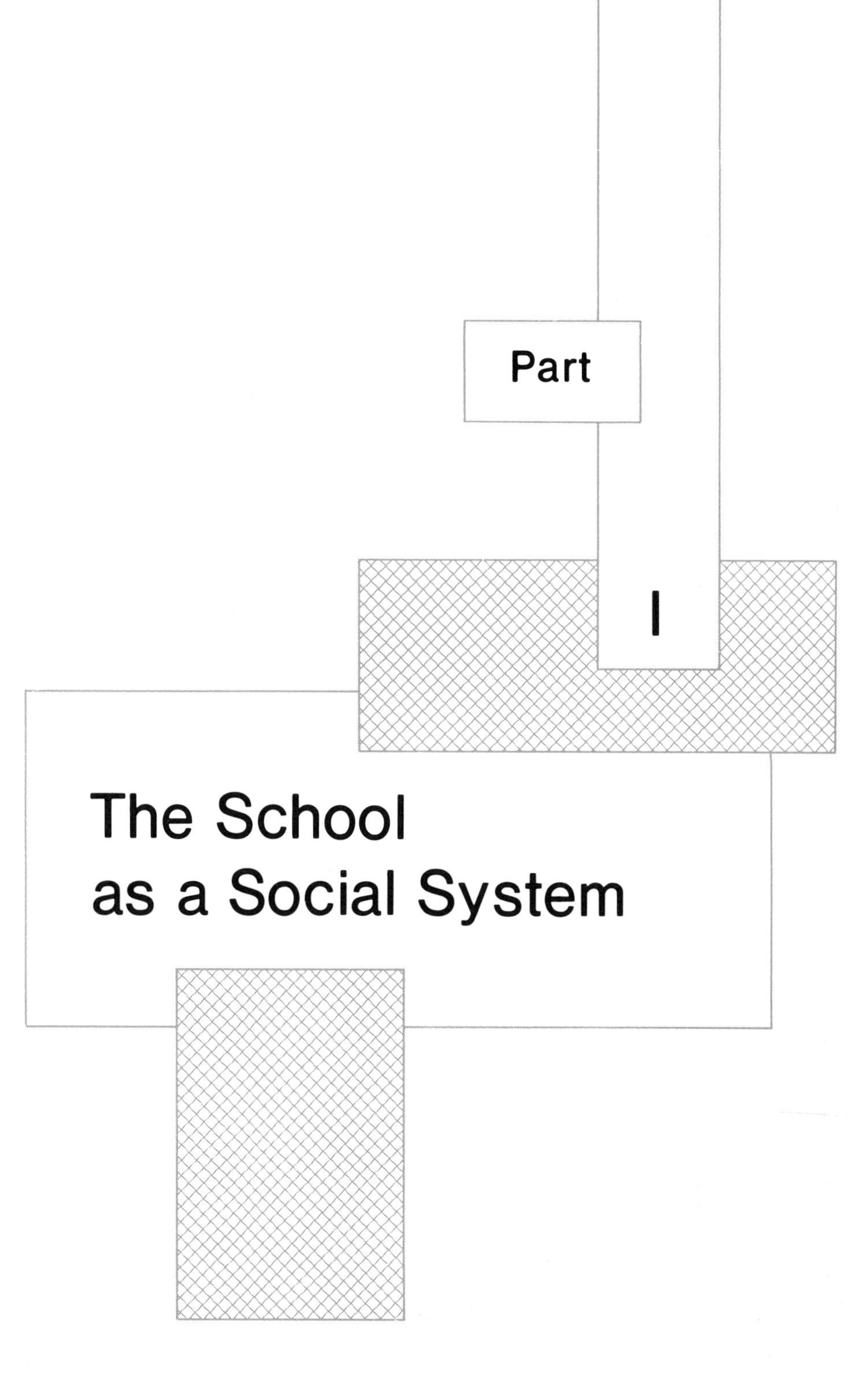

Part I

The School as a Social System

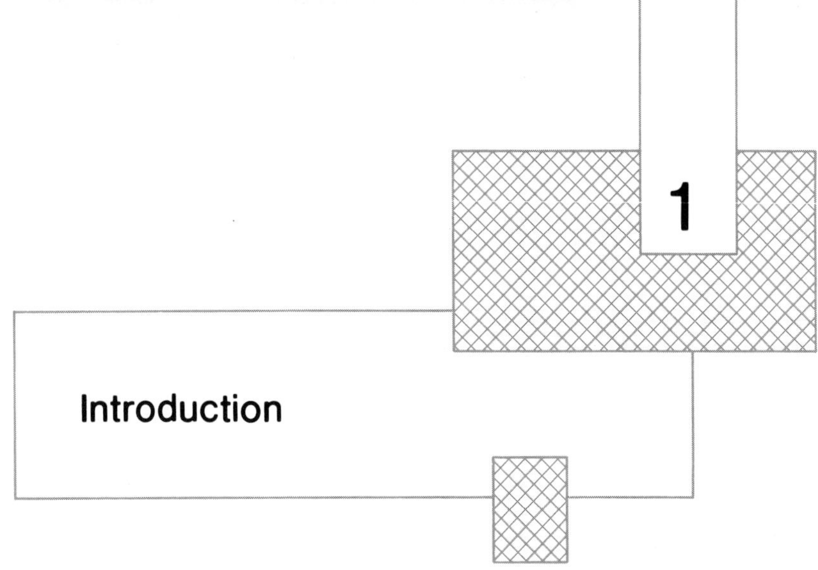

1 Introduction

Prospective teachers, now in teacher education programs, are exposed to the folklore of the profession in many different ways. The mass media present an image of the teacher and a sketchy picture of what it is like to be a teacher. Conversations with friends who have been teaching and occasional meetings with older teachers transmit more of the folklore of the profession. Student teaching, though quite different from one's first year of teaching, gives a more complete view of what it is like to be a teacher. Yet, for most prospective teachers, anxiety concerning the first year of teaching is in part the result of not knowing what to look for in order to understand the school as a social system.

What prospective teachers may profit from is an analytical framework applicable to any school system. It is the aim of this chapter to provide such a framework.

One way to understand schools is through the model of the school as a social system. The term "social system" may be used in two ways in relation to education: it may refer to the more general abstract formal education which is passed on from generation to generation or it may refer to a particular interactive social structure such as a school system in a village, suburb, or city of the United States. Within particular school systems there are also subsystems. A social studies department in a specific school provides an example of a subsystem.

The objective of this introductory chapter is to focus the attention of the reader on indicators which will help him to know what to look for in analyzing any school system. It is hoped that the reader who looks forward to his first student teaching assignment or first full-time teaching assignment will find the social system model valuable in checking preconceptions and formulating hypotheses concerning his future as a teacher.

ELEMENTS OF A SOCIAL SYSTEM

Objectives

The objectives of a social system or subsystem either reflect the changes members of the social system expect to accomplish through the operation of the system or the members' satisfaction with the status quo. Objectives may be expressed, as in the case of printed materials emanating from the central administration offices, or tacit, that is understood. The prospective teacher should look for discrepancies between expressed and tacit objectives; he should also gauge the distance between objectives, expressed or tacit, school policies, and behavior on the part of the members of the social system. A high school, for example, may have a written policy in the student handbook which states that all seniors must have the proper attitude in order to graduate. No senior, however, has been denied the right to graduate because of an improper attitude. Those teachers and administrators who are aware of the policy choose to ignore it. The behavior of the members of the social system demonstrates the fact that the policy is ineffectual. The objective, good citizenship as revealed in the student's proper attitude, remains intact in the student handbook.

The prospective teacher in search of a teaching position often experiences the shock of realizing that the objectives he has been socialized in as part of the university system are different from those subscribed to by members of a secondary school system. After recognizing that many secondary students do not go to college, the first-year teacher is gradually socialized into another social system, that of the secondary school in which he is now teaching. Most secondary teachers accept much of the new social system, thereby rejecting in large part the university system; a few do not accept the secondary school as a social system and operate as if they are still in the university system.

First-year teachers soon learn that various members of a secondary school social system often have different objectives. Some parents, for example, have as their primary goal the entrance of their son or daughter in a system of higher education; the student's teachers may feel he or she is incapable of such a venture and therefore want either to enter the world of work immediately after graduation. Other parents may not consider higher education for their child, whereas teachers encourage the student to go on for such an education.

Some first-year teachers aim at initiating innovation in a school, whereas the administrators are content with the status quo. In another school system, the administrators want to introduce innovation, while most teachers are somewhat afraid to experiment with new ideas.

Norms

Norms may be described as "rules of the game" for they describe what is considered acceptable or unacceptable in a particular social system. In some secondary schools the majority of the senior class goes on to college. Most teachers in turn look at the university professor as their prototype. Their life styles are adjusted accordingly. They see themselves as academicians, this image being more acceptable than that of other images, for example, that of the coach-athlete. Students have also accepted the norms of the social system. As good grades are a prerequisite to college entrance, there is a good deal of competition for such grades. Athletic competition is of secondary importance in this school. Administrators, subject to the pressure brought by community expectations, have built a rhetoric around past successes in getting students into first-rate colleges. Almost all of the members of this particular school as a social system have accepted the norms of the system. Their behavior indicates such an acceptance. Other secondary schools have their own norms, for the "rules of the game" vary from school to school in a decentralized system of education such as the one we have in the United States.

Status-Roles

Status-roles indicate that which is expected of a member of the social system because of his position or status in the social system. When a teacher becomes an administrator, his former colleagues say he has really changed as a person. In fact, the expectations of his new position dictate a different role in the social system. Much of the animosity and distrust among members of a school system is the result of members' failure to understand status-roles in the school as a social system. This lack of understanding leads to blanket generalizations such as "Never trust an administrator" or "Never trust a teacher." To say that one does not perform well in his status-role is different than to say that all in a particular status-role do not perform well.

Power

Power may be simply defined as control over others. There are two kinds of power: *authority* is the right as determined by the social system to control the actions of others; *influence* is control of a non-authoritative nature over others. For example, the school board, in behalf of the people of the community, gives the principal the authority to design a new curriculum in the social studies for school X. Mr. Jones, a social studies teacher at school X and lifetime friend of the principal, uses his influence to affect the principal's decisions concerning the new social studies curriculum.

Social Rank

Social rank is consensus within the social system as to what is to be rated high and what is to be rated low insofar as this is relevant to the system under consideration. If, for example, a school system feels that math and science have had their day and it is time to emphasize the social studies, it is clear that the social rank for the social studies in that school system is high at the present time.

Sanctions

Rewards (positive sanctions) and penalties (negative sanctions) are instruments used to induce compliance with the objectives and/or norms of a social system. The study of sanctions in a school system is most intriguing, for a study of rewards and penalties for teachers and students places the system in clearer perspective.

Facilities

Facilities are the means used by the social system to attain its ends or goals. Given the desire of community X to improve the social studies, what facilities are available to meet this objective? If the community wants to introduce seminars in historiography, are the teachers academically prepared to meet this challenge? Are appropriate historical sources available to reach this goal?

The prospective teacher should look at some of the following indicators in order to discover the elements of a particular social system:

School
Classrooms
Library
Audiovisual room
Counseling and nurse facilities
Cafeteria
Faculty lounge
Teaching staff (degrees, stability, dress, etc.)
Psychologist, speech therapist, and others
Administrative and office staff
Office secretaries, counseling secretaries, and custodians (their power or control of certain things)
Parents and teachers (talk to them about the school and community)
Curriculum (grouping, textbooks, etc.)
Extra curricular activities (band, vocal, athletics, dramatics, clubs)
Faculty and student handbooks
Student bulletin boards
School newspapers
Yearbook
P.T.A. (strength)
Discipline methods (punitive, corrective, consistent with learning theory)
Organizations (A.F.T., N.E.A., and others)

Physical appearance of campus
Transportation methods
Summer programs

District

District paper
District office
School board
Superintendent
Financial status of district (salary schedule)
Teacher applications and information sent to teachers

Community

Local newspapers
Personal contacts (local)
Student hangouts

Residential Areas

Business areas and types of businesses
Growth of area
Educational facilities in the community (universities, colleges, etc.)

SOCIAL CHANGE

Given the elements of a social system, how does change occur in a social system? Change may occur by changing the relative importance of different social systems in a society. It is argued by some, for example, that the school must assume many of the duties formerly held by the home. It is up to the school, the argument continues, to teach values formerly taught by the parents, for a high divorce rate and working mothers expand role expectations for the school.

A second way to achieve social change is to create new social systems and/or subsystems within social systems. Teachers may not be near a university for work beyond the bachelor's degree and so an extension service is established in the community. Some teachers may not be receptive to change; consequently, the department chairman initiates a series of seminars for those teachers interested in change. This seminar becomes the curriculum committee. A new subsystem has been created in the interest of social change.

Social change may also occur by both changing the elements of the social systems and their relation to one another and creating new elements. An informal group of teachers in a school may oppose the organization which presently represents the teachers. This informal group organizes formally and establishes a new representative body for the teachers.

As innovation is a central concern of this book, social change will be the subject of many of the following case studies. The particular processes involved in social change will be cited in the following paragraphs.

Communication

A rather well-known administrator was fired for "innovation without explanation." This is another way of saying that there was either a communication breakdown or that a "communication breakdown" acted as a rationalization for those who wanted to fire the administrator anyway. At any rate, it is generally understood that communication plays a very important part in achieving social change. Communication may be achieved through formal channels (Gesellschaft) or through informal means (Gemeinschaft). The school newspaper for parents which emanates from the administration office is an example of the former; the teacher's lounge, boiler room, and corridors are some of the places where informal communication occurs.

Decision-Making

The decision-making process in any school system is interesting to analyze. How do those in power use their authority to try to achieve change? How do those with influence but not authority initiate change—especially change not supported by those with authority? How do those who do not formally have the power use their influence to support or subvert those who want change?

Boundary Maintenance

Those within a social system try to defend their values from outside forces. Administrators, teachers, and students may band together to oppose consolidation within a school district. Such consolidation, it may be claimed, would ruin the autonomy of "Watertown High School."

Social-cultural Linkage

Social-cultural linkage is achieved when the elements of two social systems function as a unit. For example, a social studies department wants to have its students work with the city government to assure a large turnout for an election. The change system, in this case the school as represented by the social studies department, brings the proposed change to the attention of the second social system, the city government. This may be classified as *initiation.* The city government then either accepts or rejects the change initiated by the school. If the change is accepted *legitimation* is said to occur for the change is made "rightful" to the city government. The next step is *execution.* The social studies department gets the school to work together with the city government to register voters.

CONCLUSION

If we understand the elements of any social system we can comprehend any school system and its relationship to other social systems. If we understand some of the ways in which social change takes place we can comprehend any situation in which some people want to retain the status quo and others want to innovate.

The previously discussed elements of a social system and concepts involved in social change should provide the reader with an analytical framework which will be valuable in understanding the case studies which comprise the main body of this book. Each case study contains a problem situation and the reader is placed in the position of the teacher involved. You are there. What will you do?

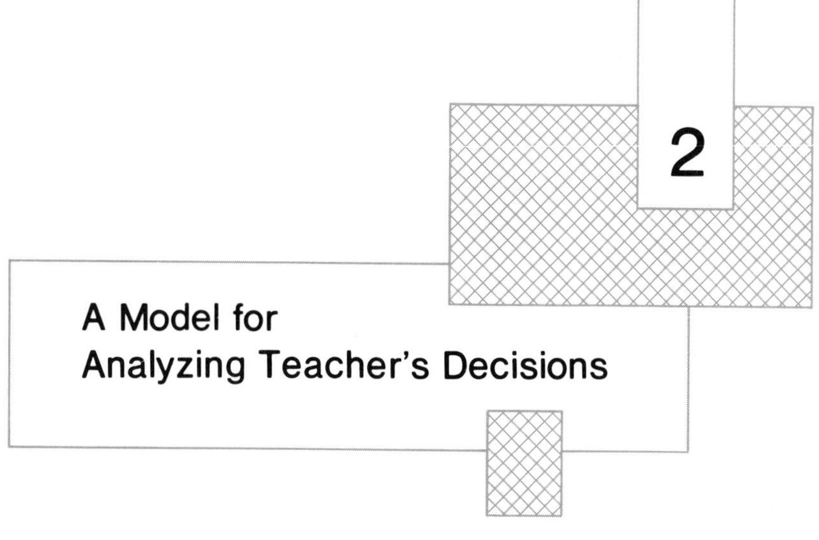

2

A Model for Analyzing Teacher's Decisions

Any decision made by a teacher is a reflection of his belief system. A teacher's beliefs are his normative value judgments, that is, what he thinks *should be* the case. The teacher, like others in our society, cannot teach without prescribing—that is, trying to convince those with whom he comes in contact of the validity of his value judgments. There are, of course, many ways to achieve consensus, some of which are more subtle and effective than others. More important, however, is the fact that teachers try to achieve consensus on a variety of subjects so that for purposes of discussion we may categorize their prescriptions. The categories or areas are not rigid or definitive and are related to each other as part of the entire educational process.

Area One—Management of Students. Prescriptions concerning the management of students are found in every classroom and school. "Put your name at the top of the paper before handing it in to the teacher" and "Raise your hand before speaking" are examples of classroom prescriptions. In the school as a whole, you might hear the following: "No roughhousing or yelling in the halls or at assemblies" or "Fighting on school grounds leads to automatic suspension."

Area Two—Student Health. Some prescriptions are considered necessary for the physical well-being of students. At a rather basic level the following advice might be given: "Put your coat on before going outside"; You should eat a good breakfast every morning." Other value judgments are based on solid empirical evidence but are frequently prescribed in moralistic "sermon-like" terms. "Smoking and drinking are evil." "Drugs are bad." (Definition of drugs not given.) Schools try to achieve consensus on these matters in a variety of ways: bulletin boards, poster contests, films, and daily announcements provide but four examples. It should be added in passing that some teachers feel that consensus on these issues is more important than looking at the issues in any kind of analytical framework.

Area Three—Aesthetics. Prescriptions concerning aesthetic matters are relevant to teaching. The teacher's value judgments as to what constitutes "good" art, music, and literature reflect his biases, biases which may or may not be based on his background and expertise in these areas. For example, one teacher asked his students to bring phonograph records to a late Friday afternoon class. When one student brought in a record by the Monkees, the teacher said, "Now, we don't play records like that in school, do we!!!" (Needless to say, an opportunity to discuss aesthetic values was missed.)

Area Four—Analysis. The teacher who advocates analysis is also prescribing. In effect, he is saying that analysis is a good thing and his students should think likewise. As Ernest E. Bayles has so aptly stated with reference to analytical situations: "The class is first maneuvered into a problem, an I-don't-know situation."[1]

Area Five—Substantive Issues. The most controversial kind of prescription is that based on the substantive values held by the teacher.[2] Should the teacher and his students analyze these values? Does the teacher have an obligation to teach some values as absolute truths? Is it desirable for a teacher to try to achieve consensus on substantive issues? Is it possible to teach values by design in classes? Let us examine the following substantive value judgments with the previous questions in mind. "Spiritual values are more important than anything else." "Totalitarianism is better than democracy." "Democracy is better than totalitarianism." "Racial desegregation is a good thing." "Racial segregation is a good thing." Which of these positions do you personally support? Which of these, if any, would you teach?

RESOLVING THE NORMATIVE-ANALYTICAL ISSUE

The thesis of this chapter is threefold: (1) Prescriptions are inevitable and can be expected from all who are interested in instruction, viz., the public, administrators, teachers, and students; (2) Teachers and their students should recognize the distinction between normative value judgments and analysis; and (3) The way in which the teachers' prescriptions are made is usually more important than the particular prescription advocated by the teacher.

---

[1]Ernest E. Bayles, *Democratic Educational Theory,* Harper & Row, Publishers, New York, 1960, p. 189.

[2]The term "substantive" is borrowed from Edwin Fenton, *Teaching the New Social Studies in Secondary Schools,* Holt, Rinehart & Winston, Inc., New York, 1966, p. 42.

Prescriptions Are Inevitable. Occasionally one meets a teacher who feels that his teaching is objective and all sides of any issue are heard in his classroom. George S. Counts spoke of this issue in his classic work, *Dare the School Build a New Social Order?* "It is obvious that the whole of creation cannot be brought into the school. This means that some selection must be made of teachers, curricula, architecture, methods of teaching. And in the making of the selection, the dice must always be weighted in favor of this or that."[3] Students are quick to realize the mood of their teacher on any given issue. Inflection in one's voice, facial expressions, and choice of vocabulary may indicate how the teacher feels about a particular issue.

The inevitability of prescriptions by all parties interested in our schools should be understood by students as well as their teachers. It is certainly legitimate for students to analyze legislation which directly influences their formal education. In California, for example, the teacher is legally required to train pupils in morality, manners, and citizenship.

> Each teacher shall endeavor to impress upon the minds of the pupils the principles of morality, truth, justice, patriotism, and a true comprehension of the rights, duties, and dignity of American citizenship, to teach them to avoid idleness, profanity, and falsehood, and to instruct them in manners and morals and the principles of a free government.[4]

Let us imagine, for the moment, that a teacher feels that the part of the California Code cited above is not only chauvinistic but also irrelevant. That is, it is extremely patriotic and an example of the outdated Protestant Ethic. His human judgment is now at least overtly in conflict with legalism. What alternatives are open to him? He may openly defy the legislation, telling those around him that the law is ridiculous. In the process he may make his views known to his legislative representatives. He will probably lose his job in the process for the community will, in this matter, rush to the support of the law. His principal, legally accountable for enforcing the Education Code, cannot support the teacher. A second alternative is for the teacher to try to go through legal channels, including the principal, in order to make his views known without openly defying the law. A third alternative, one commonly practiced by teachers who disagree with such legislation, is to simply ignore the particular law and go about the business of teaching. This is but one example of the conflict in teaching between legalism and human judgment.

The teacher rarely finishes a day of teaching without facing the conflict between legalism and human judgment several times. He drives

---

[3]George S. Counts, *Dare the School Build a New Social Order?* The John Day Company, Inc., New York, 1932, p. 19.

[4]Education Code. Sacramento, California: State of California, 1963. vol. I, p. 356.

his car into the school parking lot, gets out of his car, and glances to his right only to find that there are several students smoking in their car. The school rule reads "NO SMOKING ON SCHOOL GROUNDS!" Will the teacher face this situation directly by taking the students to the principal's office, indirectly by reporting them to the principal, or simply ignore the students?

During the day a student reports to the teacher that some students have been smoking marijuana in the restroom. What course will the teacher take in order to deal with this matter? A second student may confidentially relate to the teacher that her father had beaten her at home that morning thus accounting for her inattention in class. Should the teacher relate this to authorities and see what legal action can be taken or simply keep this information to himself?

The teacher knows that open-housing ordinances are part of the state's legal code and yet he also knows that no Blacks have been hired in his school in large part because it would be virtually impossible for Blacks to find housing in the community. Once again the teacher's judgment may conflict with legalism (in the event that he opposes Blacks moving into the community), or else conflict with the community (in the event that he supports the open-housing ordinance).

A SECOND LOOK AT OUR MODEL FOR ANALYSIS

Area One. All teachers would probably agree that some classroom management rules are necessary. There are, of course, different ways to establish rules and also different ways to interpret and enforce rules. The various ways in which the rules are constructed, interpreted, and enforced influence behavior in class and in the school as a whole. Whether students identify with the school system or feel alienated from the system will affect other levels of prescriptions made by the teacher.[5] The following example will demonstrate how prescriptions concerning the management of students may influence children in other areas of the educational process.

Sue Jackson is a seventh grade student at Central Junior High School. During the first week of school her teacher announced that at the end of the week the students would visit the library for an entire period. On Friday the students left their regular classroom and went to the library. The librarian and teacher spent the whole hour on library rules. What was Sue's reaction?

---

[5]This matter is discussed at length in the excellent book, *Society's Children: A Study of Ressentiment in the Secondary School,* by Carl Nordstrom, Edgar Z. Friedenberg, and Hilary A. Gold. New York: Random House, 1967.

"When my teacher said that we would go to the library at the end of the week I was very excited. I've gone to the city library with mother and had a great time looking around and checking out my own books. When Friday came and we went to the school library I was very disappointed. The teacher and librarian spent the entire period telling us a bunch of rules that I can't even remember now. The school library and city library sure are different."

The teacher's classroom teaching may be influenced by discipline in the school as a whole. If, for example, the teacher becomes emotionally involved in disciplining a student at an assembly or in the halls his temper may be short in the next class he teaches or for the remainder of his classes during the day.

It should be added that there is a connection between teachers who are obsessed with maintaining discipline in our schools and political conservatism. In other words, those teachers who want a great deal more school discipline accentuate the authority role of the teacher to the exclusion of inquiry and self-expression in the school. Consensus on those matters deemed patriotic and moral becomes more important than inquiry and analysis. Who are these teachers? According to Harmon Zeigler, they are primarily males rather than females. Zeigler argues that most males become more conservative and authoritarian because they do not like their work. They do not like their work because they are in an establishment basically considered feminine by the public, an establishment with relatively low income, and an establishment where hope for advancement fades with experience.[6]

That the matter of discipline is central in the eyes of many teachers becomes obvious in conversations with teachers. We may better understand the term "discipline" by examining five concepts of discipline proposed by William C. Bagley in his book *School Discipline.*[7]

The first is the concept of original sin. That is, there is an evil spirit within the child that makes him misbehave. The answer to his sinful nature is vindictive punishment. Retribution must be imposed. Corporal punishment is the answer. The following comments describe this view of discipline: "I know I used to do that. All children do. A good spanking occasionally keeps them in line"; "He's full of the devil. Just like all the kids. I've always said, 'Spare the rod and spoil the child' "; "Man is born selfish. He's no different. A good whipping will take care of that."

---

[6]Harmon Ziegler, *The Political Life of American Teachers,* Prentice-Hall, Inc., New York, 1967, pp. 11-30.

[7]William C. Bagley, *School Discipline,* Macmillan Co., New York, 1916, pp. 179-185. The present author has discussed concepts of discipline rather than trying to define "discipline" as research indicates that there are multifarious definitions of the word. Peter F. Oliva. "High School Discipline in American Society." *Bulletin of the National* Association of Secondary-School Principals. 40: pp. 5-6, January 1956.

The second concept of discipline advocates proportionate discipline. Fit the punishment to the crime, it is argued. The following rules in a school reveal this philosophy. "One hour of detention for littering the school ground"; "Defying a teacher results in a swat with the shoe and two hours' detention"; "Fighting on school grounds brings two days' suspension plus a talk to your parents"; "Smoking on school grounds results in a week's suspension."

A third way of viewing discipline is as protective punishment. Both the offender and society must be protected. A teacher may relate, "He can't attend any more dances at school. Since he may hurt other students and himself, this is the only way to deal with this problem." A second teacher may say, "We had to send him to a detention camp. He couldn't be trusted at school and anyway, this will give him a chance to work this out for himself. It's the best thing for everybody."

A fourth way of approaching the matter of discipline is to view it as reformatory punishment aimed at the rehabilitation of the individual to society. "A year at the reform school will change his outlook on stealing"; "He'll stay in the hall and when he learns to behave himself he can come back to class"; "A few nights' detention will make him see the importance of school rules." Such statements support the concept of discipline as reformatory punishment.

A final concept of discipline advocates the prevention of misbehavior through positive approaches. Wholesome activities and self-control are emphasized. Some of the following statements support this conception of punishment. "Lower-class students tend to get into trouble. What we need is an athletic program that will let them get rid of their aggression in a good way." "Student council gives them a chance to express themselves and stand up for their own ideas." "The good thing about homework is that it keeps the kids out of trouble."

As William C. Bagley points out, all five concepts of discipline are prevalent in our schools today with some adaptations. Combinations of these concepts also exist in the schools.

Although more research on discipline is needed, the following generalizations may be made on the basis of research already conducted.[8]

1. The majority of teachers feel that they not only have an important voice in determining discipline policies in their classroom and school but also in their school system.

---

[8]The author would refer the reader to two main sources in dealing with the matter of discipline, both of which were drawn on heavily in this section of the chapter. National Education Association, Research Division. "Teacher Opinion on Pupil Behavior, 1955-56." *Research Bulletin.* Washington, D.C., 34: pp. 51-107, April 1956; and National Education Association, Research Division. "Discipline in the Public Schools." *Research Bulletin.* Washington, D.C., 35, December 1957.

2. In neighborhoods that teachers consider to be "good" a large proportion of students are classified as exceptionally well-behaved, whereas in slum areas very few students are classified as exceptionally well-behaved. Corporal punishment is also considered more appropriate in slum areas than in "good" neighborhoods.
3. The advocation of corporal punishment by many adults meets their psychic needs and so the adolescent becomes the scapegoat for their displaced aggression.
4. The populace becomes concerned with juvenile delinquency after repetitive acts of such delinquency rather than as a preventive measure with attention given to previous signs that lead to the delinquency.
5. There is a marked tendency to treat delinquency as if it takes place in a vacuum rather than considering the environmental factors which aided the delinquency.
6. Discipline is almost always imposed from outside the offender and rarely involves the offender directly in a program for his rehabilitation.

One can see from the previously cited generalizations that all of those involved in the process of education have a great distance to travel in improving our discipline in the schools. The author would suggest in closing this section of the chapter that we would do well to be concerned with:

1. Being consistent in our attitudes towards discipline as guidance not punishment. (Punishment being simply one technique in guidance.)
2. Recognizing unique problems involved in correcting maldeveloping behavior as opposed to guiding "normal" development, e.g.,
   a. breaking down attitudes
   b. rebuilding new attitudes at the same time. (We must recognize how social acceptance and social interests can assist in both these processes.)
3. Utilizing activities and positive sanctions where they can be shown to have educational value consistent with the definition of discipline. (Activities are excellent for promoting a healthy personality development if strong guidance is given.)
4. Utilizing negative sanctions where they can be shown to have educational value consistent with the definition of discipline. (This would involve an evaluation of our negative sanctions.)
5. An awareness of the importance of the *time factor*.
   a. our overall plans in terms of our expectations.
   b. how the child responds to time—how he sees it.
6. Maximum benefit in specific personality guidance is best achieved through interest and *communication* of these agencies: teachers, parents, administrators, counselors, and activity advisors.[9]

Area Two. On the basic level, prescriptions such as "You should eat a good breakfast every morning" are understandable and seemingly legitimate. This admits, however, the importance of the way in which the

[9]Dennis L. Sonnenburg, "Discipline in Our Schools." Unpublished manuscript. University of California, Santa Barbara, 1969.

teacher makes his prescription. The general tone of the teacher's prescriptions in this area will influence the rapport between the teacher and his students.

Prescriptions such as "Smoking and drinking are evil" may be criticized because they limit dialogue between the teacher and his students. The epistemological questions of how one knows what he knows and how various evidence is weighed are lost because of the teacher's desire for consensus at all costs.

Area Three. The teacher who believes that consensus is more important than inquiry on aesthetic matters also loses the opportunity to discuss judgments in any kind of analytical framework. On what basis do people make judgments concerning art, music, and literature? What are the various criteria for such judgments?

A teacher's value judgments concerning aesthetics are not confined to the classroom. Unlike some other professions, teaching demands close contact with the same people day after day in the same building. These close working conditions stimulate conflicts between teachers—conflicts which are sometimes based on aesthetic disagreement. For example, some teachers may criticize fellow colleagues for their style of clothing. Older women may feel that a young woman has her dress too short or young men may joke about the older style of clothing worn by some of their colleagues. When the author was a supervisor of student teachers, a master teacher objected because a young lady wore a wig. He felt this was in poor taste.

Teachers may also disagree as to the aesthetic value of books assigned in their colleagues' classes. Such differences often go beyond intellectual disagreement to vindictiveness which spreads throughout the school. Students become pawns in such arguments. They quickly discern areas of disagreement between teachers—especially if such disagreement results in personality conflicts.

A final example will illustrate disagreement as to aesthetic matters in our schools. An art teacher who had been teaching for many years had traditionally served as a jury of one to determine what art objects would enter the spring art festival. She would not allow any art that was "modern," much to the dismay of students and other teachers.

Area Four. As mentioned previously, the teacher who advocates analysis is prescribing. When the teacher lists tools of analysis without letting his students criticize such a list, he is on dangerous ground. The student should, for example, be able to question whether or not statistical evidence is more valid than a particular person's testimonial in dealing with an issue. Discussion in classes concerning the various tools of analysis used by scholars may well be the most neglected area of present day instruction.[10] The various uses of informants, observation, interviews, documents, and statistical findings are probably not discussed in most classes.

Area Five. The results of a rather simple role playing experiment will demonstrate the complexity of the normative–analytical issue with respect to substantive issues. The experiment also demonstrates the importance of the manner in which the teacher's prescriptions are made. The experiment was designed to allow the observer an opportunity to study the distinction teachers make, or fail to make, between their personal belief systems (normative value judgments) and the more analytical framework provided by the social sciences.

A teacher in the university class was asked to leave the room and then return in the role of a twelfth-grade teacher of a problems of democracy class. Upon entering the room the teacher was asked to read the following from a card:

> Today we want to discuss the situation in Watts in particular and the situation in city slums and ghettos in general. Do any of you know why some Negroes live in a slum area?

A fellow teacher, playing the role of a twelfth-grade student, responded as follows:

> The problem with "niggers" is that they want to get good jobs but are lazy and dirty. They just want a hand-out.

Certain common reaction patterns on the part of the teacher occurred.

1. The teacher decides consciously or otherwise, whether or not he wants to deal with the antagonist's response. One teacher, for example, said, "That's interesting. Now let's turn to our assignment for today on page. . . ."

   (The following responses occurred when teachers decided to deal with the issue rather than run from it.)

2. The teacher disagrees with the antagonist's statement and asks the student to elaborate, hoping that the "ridiculous" nature of his position will be evident as the student continues. (The teacher admitted that he hoped that the student would take enough rope to hang himself, that is express himself in an inarticulate way thereby demonstrating his stupidity to the rest of the class.) The teacher encouraged elaboration by asking, "Exactly what do you mean when you say the Negro is dirty and lazy?"

3. The teacher became very emotional and preached a sermon to the antagonist so that the student was forced to retreat in silence. "You

[10]The following sources may be valuable to the reader in dealing with inquiry. *The Tools of Social Science.* Garden City, N. Y.: Anchor Books, 1965; and E. J. Webb *et. al. Unobtrusive Research in the Social Sciences.* Chicago: Rand McNally & Co., 1966.

know we don't use that kind of language in here. The Negro is every bit as good as the white man. Look at Ralph Bunche for example. . . ." Obviously any kind of dialogue between protagonist and antagonist did not occur.

4. The most common response was for the teacher to throw the issue back to the class as a whole—the teacher hoping that other members of the class would refute the antagonist's statement: "Who disagrees with this point of view? I wonder if any of you feel differently on this subject." If no member of the class refuted the antagonist, the teacher, feeling very strongly about the subject, would frequently assign the antagonist special reading or set up a special unit on the Negro in American history.

It should be clear from the previous example and discussion of the five areas that the way in which the teacher's prescriptions are made is extremely important. Dialogue may be fostered or stifled depending on the manner in which the teacher approaches controversial issues.

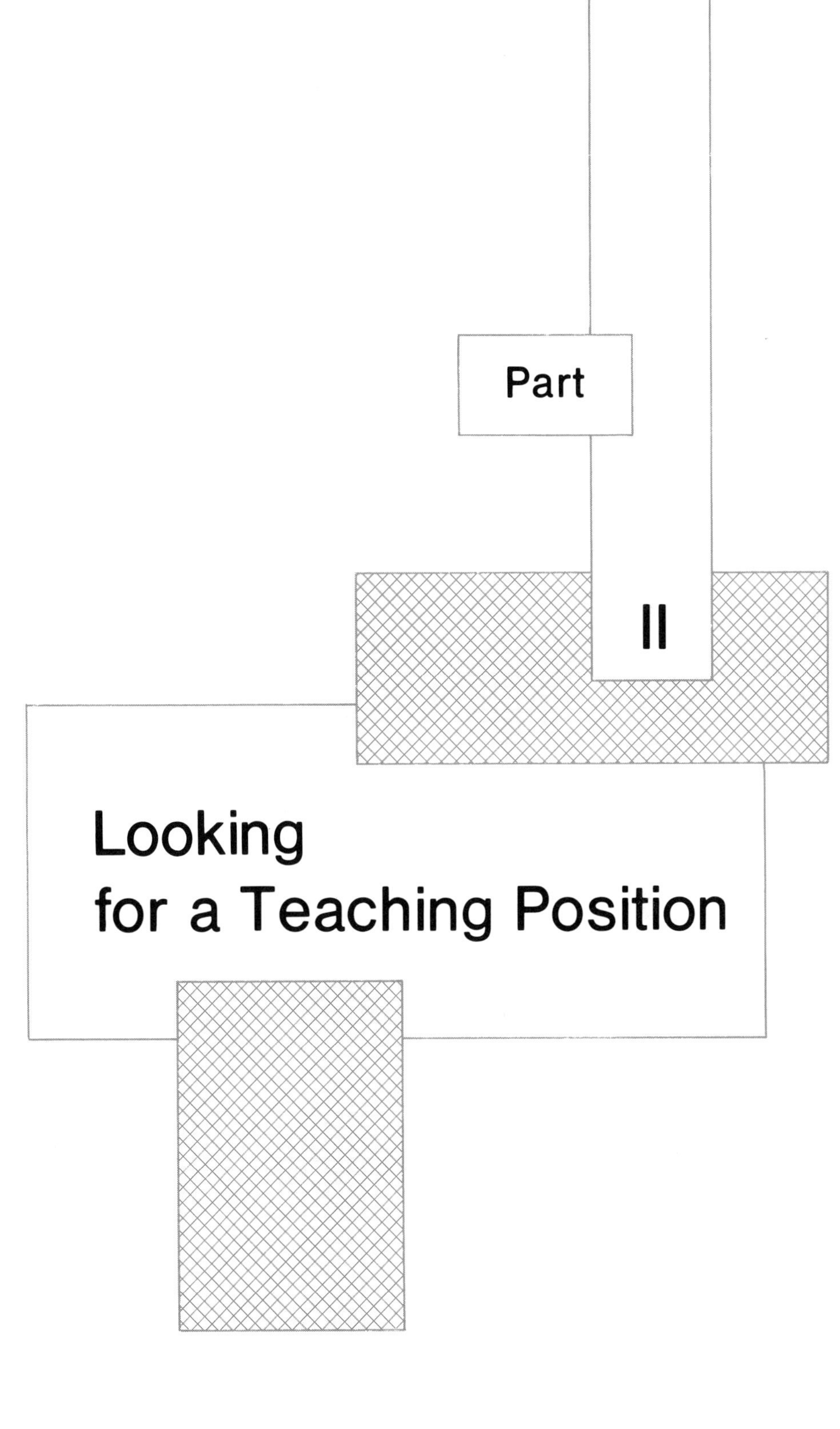

Part

II

Looking for a Teaching Position

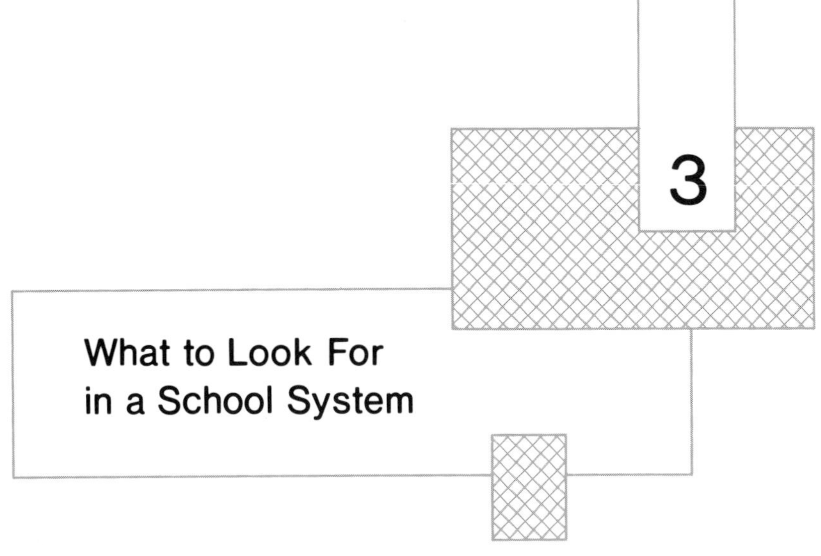

3 What to Look For in a School System

How flattering it is to receive your first teaching offer from a school system! As a college student you may well have experienced financial hardship or at least it would be safe to say that you were not the recipient of full-time wages. In any case, when an offer is made in a letter, on a phone, or via a conversation, it is indeed hard to believe that someone is actually going to pay you to teach. Perhaps the lack of pay for most student teaching experiences makes your salary offer especially gratifying.

But before you receive an invitation to join a school's faculty you will probably have been interviewed at a college or university placement center and/or the school where the vacancy for which you applied exists. It should, therefore, be worth our time to discuss both interview situations with an eye to the factors which will determine whether or not you would enjoy teaching in a particular school system, and in turn whether or not they would appreciate your teaching.

INTERVIEWING AT A COLLEGE OR UNIVERSITY PLACEMENT CENTER

Initial contacts by school systems with teaching candidates are increasingly being made at campus placement centers. As teacher education programs and school systems become larger, the importance of campus placement centers should increase. In fact, if one looks at colleges and universities around the nation he can see the expansion of interviewing facilities.

Announcements as to which school systems are interviewing at what times will be available at department offices and the placement center itself. The crucial question is, "What are the factors which will help you decide whether or not you want to be interviewed by a particular school system?"

Tradition

Like it or not, what you are used to plays a part in your decision to interview. Where you were born, raised, or went to college, may cause you to choose a school system nearby as you will probably feel most comfortable in such a school system. At the same time, there are many students who want to reject their tradition and go to the other end of the country, if not another country, to try something different.

Expectations and Desires of Parents

Although the student does not like to admit it, his parents usually exert a considerable influence on him. Many students are tempted to return to their home town to teach, reminded by their parents' invitation to enjoy free room if not board. Other students will move across the nation to avoid the influence of their parents.

Influence of Close College Friends

It is rather common for young unmarried students to have their first full-time teaching experience at the same school chosen by a close friend or friends. There are obvious social advantages to having your old friends in the same area.

Location

Climate plays a part in most candidates' decisions as to where they want to teach. "Go west, young man, go west" is still the cry of many easterners who are tired of snow. At the same time, those who enjoy easily accessible ski areas and the changing seasons one experiences in the Midwest and East are not interested in living in the West. Do you want to be near a university to do graduate work? If so, this will influence your choice of location.

Junior High School or High School Vacancy

Most candidates have a preference as to whether they want to teach at the junior or senior high school level. Many school systems will simply interview the candidate for a secondary position and then later place him in either junior or senior high school teaching.

Size of the School System and Community in Which It Is Located

Do you want to teach in a rural, suburban, or urban area? Do you want to teach in a school with 200 students or 2,000 students? You may feel more comfortable in a community similar to that in which you were raised or you may wish to experience the challenge of a community whose size is entirely foreign to you.

General Tone of the School and the School System's Location

What is the socioeconomic background of the student body and the people who live near the school site? How will this influence you as to whether or not you choose a school? Unless you have had experience in a school system you must rely in large part on rumors and hearsay in answering many of these questions.

Salary Schedule

What candidates hear about different schools' salary schedules and fringe benefits will determine to some extent whether or not they decide to be interviewed at the campus placement center.

Occupation of Spouse

This factor is especially crucial to a young woman. If, for example, her husband is going on to graduate school, she will be limited in her choice of school systems to those in the immediate area of the graduate school which her husband chooses.

You should be able to name several other factors which are important to you at the campus placement center. The list above is but an indication as to the variables involved.

When you go to the placement center you should realize that very few jobs are offered at this particular interview. In fact, some campus placement centers advise the interviewer not to make any definite offers. Instead, an initial contact is made at this interview and if both parties are amenable to each other a second interview is arranged at the school where the teaching position exists.

The interviewer on campus will probably be a personnel representative from the school system rather than a principal from the school with the vacancy. Because of this the interviewer's questions are usually more general in nature than those asked by the principal who will conduct the second interview. The following questions are typical of the questions you may expect from the personnel representative who will be interviewing you:

What is your philosophy of education?
Why do you want to be a teacher?
What made you decide to become a teacher?
How did you enjoy student teaching?
What are your professional and educational teaching goals?
Describe your favorite high school teacher.
What activities were you engaged in during your college career?
What experiences have you had working with children?
What are you looking for in selecting a school where you want to teach?

What is the reason for these general questions asked by the interviewer? Quite simply, he wants to know whether or not you should be considered as a serious candidate, i.e., should you be invited for a second interview to be held at the school. The basic question the interviewer and the principal have in mind is, would you be compatible with the particular school system? Would you be able to get along with your colleagues, the administration, and the students? Whether a school system should in fact consider your ability to "get along" as the main basis for hiring is a questionable matter; however, it is important that you understand that this fact is paramount in many interviewers' minds.

Half of the job of the interviewer at the campus placement center is to appraise you; the other half of his job is to sell his school system to the person being interviewed. He may well spend the first part of the interview talking to you about his school system and the community in which it is located. This introduction may also be designed to put you at ease. A rather interesting development is occurring in university interviewing: audiovisual materials, such as slides and even movies, are being used to impress the candidate.

A major question is in the candidate's mind as he prepares for and participates in the interviewing situation: "Should I really be honest or should I try to play the game in order to get the job?" It is the author's belief that your candid opinions, tentative though they might be, should be given to the interviewer. It is very important that you teach in a school system which will allow you to develop those ideas which are of great importance to you. If you compromise too much in the interview it is quite possible that you will do likewise in your teaching. The real losers will not only be you but your students.

INTERVIEWING AT THE SCHOOL IN WHICH YOU ARE INTERESTED

You have now been invited, probably by letter or perhaps even at the end of the interview at the university placement center, to visit the school where there is a vacancy. The principal who greets you will try to put you at ease through a variety of methods. For example, he may take you around the school and introduce you to your prospective colleagues. After this initial introduction and general discussion the principal will probably ask you certain questions which will determine whether or not he will ultimately invite you to teach at his school. Some of the following case studies deal with problem situations principals will pose for you. Other case studies identify various problems which may occur as you seek a teaching position.

Case Study Number 3-1

YOUR REACTION TO A CONTROVERSIAL SUPERINTENDENT

You have an interview with Mr. Jones, the superintendent of White County. Upon entering the room, you introduce yourself and inform him of the scheduled interview. He then proceeds to hunt for your portfolio which was sent to him almost two months ago. Upon finding your file he looks through it saying, "I didn't get a chance to look at this before. What kind of a job do you want?" You inform him you have applied for a teaching position in his district. He is silent for a moment and then comments, "That's nice. What are your qualifications?" At this time the phone rings and the following ensues: "Hello. What the hell do you want? She went where? Doesn't she realize we are interviewing people for jobs this week? Who the hell does she think she is anyway! You call her and tell her I want her back at her desk in one hour or she will hear plenty from me. Damn her anyway, does she think she owns the school or something? I don't care about her other appointments. You tell her in one hour!! I'm sending a prospective teacher to see her and by God she had better be there when he arrives. Got that?" As he hangs up he remarks to you, "These damn administrators. They think they own the schools or something. They are just working for me and the sooner they realize that the better. She had better shape up fast or she will be looking for another job."

You are handed a piece of paper with an address. After giving you directions on how to find the school, he dismisses you summarily without rising or even saying goodbye.

You go to the designated school and have to wait for the assistant principal to return from her doctor's appointment. Upon her arrival, the interview proceeds smoothly and you are relieved to find that she is a warm, friendly person who seems to be genuinely interested in your personal and professional welfare.

After your conversation, you are requested to return to the superintendent's office for an additional interview with Mr. Jones. If he and the assistant principal feel you qualify, you will be notified.

What will your reaction be at this point?

Case Study Number 3-2

SUPERINTENDENT NOT THERE FOR INTERVIEW

You are a new teacher and have received an invitation to an interview with the superintendent. You arrive a little early and take a chair in the outer office. When the time for the appointment passes, the secretary informs you that the superintendent is out and will be in shortly. One and one-half hours later you ask what chances you will have to see the superintendent. You are assured that he will want to see you.

How would you react?

Case Study Number 3-3

PRIVATE COLLEGE VS. STATE COLLEGE

During your interview for a teaching position your interviewer compares your trip to Europe with his. Then he asks you about your qualifications. You tell him that you went to a private school. For fifteen minutes he tells you about the time he went to college and how he saved his parents a lot of money by going to a state school.

What will your reaction be?

Case Study Number 3-4

YOUR REACTION TO APPARENT IGNORANCE ON THE PART OF THE INTERVIEWER

During an employment interview for a position to teach in a secondary school, the principal tells you about his school's program in your subject field. In his enthusiasm, he makes statements about your subject which are false.

How do you react to this confusion?

Case Study Number 3-5

SCHOOL CONSERVATISM

You are being interviewed by the principal of a school at which you had hoped to be a teacher. The principal is an elderly man who quickly lets you know his personal conservatism and the conservatism of the school administration. He tells you that no nonsense will be tolerated. You personally are very liberally oriented and have grand ideas of revolutionizing the education process.

What do you do?

Case Study Number 3-6

YOUR REACTION TO THE PRINCIPAL'S REMARKS ABOUT FRATERNIZATION WITH WOMEN STUDENTS (Male Teacher)

You are interviewing. Almost as an aside, the principal adds, "By the way, there should be no socializing with any of your female students."

What will your reaction be?

Case Study Number 3-7
YOUR VIEW OF DISCIPLINE ASKED

When applying for a position, the interviewing administrator breaks from the normal questioning and very directly asks: "What is your approach to discipline?"

How do you answer?

Case Study Number 3-8
INTERVIEWER SPENDS MOST OF THE TIME QUESTIONING APPLICANT ABOUT DISCIPLINARY PROCEDURES

You are an experienced teacher applying for a job in another school district. The interviewer at this meeting spends most of the time asking you about your own thoughts regarding discipline and corporal punishment and some of your own practices in your former school. It is readily apparent that he believes in "running a tight ship," that there should be no "monkey business," and that he expects the teachers he hires to be strict disciplinarians. You, however, happen to believe that many aspects of education, such as interpersonal relations and creative expression, are encouraged best in a freer atmosphere.

What do you say in response to his questions?

Case Study Number 3-9
YOUR REACTION TO AN OPPOSING VIEW OF TEACHING

You are a prospective teacher who wants to teach secondary art. You have your own convictions as to how the subject should be taught in the classroom. Art is subjective and cannot be taught in a typical classroom situation where there are neat and orderly rows of desks and chairs and where there is absolute silence and strict discipline. Your objective is to generate a creative spirit and individual exploration in the classroom.

You have an interview with Mr. Jones, the principal of Maroon High School. There is a position open at the school for the ensuing year. The interview goes quite well at the beginning. You are impressed with the excellent school facilities, the location and size of the school, and the salary. Then Mr. Jones discusses his point of view on teaching art: "You know, I don't think that teachers are stressing the important aspects of art anymore. There should be less freedom and more crafts in the art classes. Neatness and good control are important things in the classroom. Don't you think so?"

How will you react to this statement?

Case Study Number 3-10

YOUR RESPONSE TO THE ADMINISTRATOR WHO SAYS HE WILL NOT HIRE A TEACHER WHO USES THE NEW APPROACH TO YOUR SUBJECT

You are a prospective teacher full of enthusiasm for the new method you have seen used effectively and are confronted by a hiring principal who resents the approach for reasons he considers valid. The principal says he will not hire a teacher who uses this approach and asks you what method you plan to use.

What will your answer be?

Case Study Number 3-11

CONTROVERSY CONCERNING TRACKING OF STUDENTS ON BASIS OF TEST SCORES

In applying for a position as a high school teacher, you are informed that part of your job will be concerned with "placing" students in some classes solely on the basis of test scores from a widely used test. You are aware that the high school population does not reflect the normative sample used for the reliability and validity studies of the test producer. The principal is concerned with placing students in classes so that there is little overt dissatisfaction from students or parents. Test scores are used to defend placement. You have strong feelings concerning the possibility of "tracking" students on the basis of test scores.

What would you do?

Case Study Number 3-12

INTERVIEW PROBLEM CONCERNING PRESSURE FROM ATHLETE

You are a prospective teacher applying for a position in a very sportsminded community high school. Here is the situation proposed to you during an interview. What would you do?

Danny is a high school senior who is a very athletic young man, but does very poorly scholastically. Danny has no discipline problems and has been socially promoted for three years to play basketball, football, and track.

Danny has been offered a scholarship to attend the university next fall. Of course the university is under the impression his grades meet specifications. The grade that you give Danny is the determining factor.

What is your reaction?

Case Study Number 3-13

QUESTION ABOUT THE UNFAMILIAR

You are interviewing for a job that you want very much. The interviewer asks you a question about something with which you are totally unfamiliar.

What would your response be?

Case Study Number 3-14

POLICY CONCERNING FEMALE TEACHERS WHO ARE ALSO MOTHERS

This applies only to female teachers. You are coming to the end of an interview for a position that you feel has more to offer than you possibly hoped for. The size of the class, the type of student, the latitude you are given as to what you teach, all seem to approach perfection. You are about to sign the contract when the principal says, "Oh, by the way, I notice you have two young children. We have a policy at our school that teachers who are mothers must make provision for the care of the children when they are ill. Otherwise, as you can see, we would be constantly obliged to find substitutes."

How will you respond?

Case Study Number 3-15

LACK OF SPECIFIC TEACHING SCHEDULE

You are impressed with the looks of a particular community, have sent in an application, and are called for an interview. Everything is fine until you ask what your schedule would be and what classes you would be expected to teach (your major field? minor field? both?). The interviewer replies that he cannot really be sure what or how much you would be teaching but that you could have the job. You remember you have heard others mentioning six or seven classes a day, teaching two or three subjects.

What would you say?

Case Study Number 3-16

JUNIOR HIGH JOB VS. HIGH SCHOOL JOB

You have been told by a friend, who knows that you wish to change teaching positions, that a teaching job has suddenly become available in his district about the end of June. However, it is in a junior high school and you are most interested in high school teaching. You arrange an interview with the principal, and after you have discussed the job and your qualifications, he asks you about your interest in junior high school and whether you think you would like to stay in teaching at that level.

What is your answer?

Case Study Number 3-17
TEACHING IN MINOR RATHER THAN MAJOR

You have applied for a junior high school position late in August. The principal explains that they desperately need someone to teach four classes in your minor and one class in your major. The cause for the varied assignment is the relatively small size of the school.

What would you do?

Case Study Number 3-18
ONE CLASS AND FOUR STUDY HALLS

You have requested a teaching position in a culturally-advantaged neighborhood. The only opening available in this area is for one class in your major and four study halls.

What will your reaction be?

Case Study Number 3-19
ASKED TO TEACH FAMILY LIFE COURSE

You apply for a social studies teaching position in a large high school. All seems acceptable for your appointment on the part of both parties until the administrator introduces you to your department head. He remarks "How glad I am we found someone to teach that Family Life course." You do not feel well qualified to teach a "Family Life" course.

What is your reaction?

Case Study Number 3-20
SACRIFICING IDEALS VERSUS A CHOICE AREA FOR TEACHING

You are applying for a job teaching in a high school. You have narrowed your choice down to two high schools, each of which has offered you a position. One is in a lower-middle-class area with an average salary but with a principal known to be liberal minded toward giving his faculty a relatively free hand in their teaching. The other is in an upper-middle-class area with a slight increase in salary and a principal known to be adamant on the idea that teachers must do exactly as he wishes; furthermore, that all serious disciplinary problems must be handled only after checking with him first.

What will your reaction be?

Case Study Number 3-21

URBAN GHETTO SCHOOL VERSUS SUBURBAN SCHOOL

You have arrived in Los Angeles late in August for your final interview for a teaching position in their secondary system. You have just traveled 2,000 miles from back East with your wife and family and this was your only lead for a job. You were informed in the interview that all of the high school positions in the region of Los Angeles, where you preferred to teach, were filled. They promptly informed you that there was available a 7th grade position in the Watts area or a 7th grade position in San Pedro (a culturally advantaged school). This was your first year of teaching and all of your training was in high school grades. You have to make the decision by the next day.

With this dilemma facing you and under pressure of time, what are you to do?

Case Study Number 3-22

PRINCIPAL QUESTIONS YOUR ABILITY TO TEACH CHILDREN FROM LOWER SOCIOECONOMIC LEVELS

You have taught successfully in a high economic level community for several years. You are now seeking a position in a public school in a lower-income area. The principal questions your ability to understand, to communicate, and to handle children from the lower social and economic levels. He feels your experience in the sheltered atmosphere of your previous school does not qualify you for the job. He feels that teaching children of lower-income groups is much more demanding than teaching well-motivated children from economically secure families. You want the job and you feel equipped for it.

How do you handle this man's doubts about your ability?

Case Study Number 3-23

YOU ARE OFFERED TWO TEACHING POSITIONS AFTER SERVING AS A "VISTA" VOLUNTEER

After a year with VISTA, you have two teaching opportunities. The first offer is a middle-class suburban school in an all-white community. The second school offers a lower salary schedule; however, it appeals to your educational interests as it is comprised of a high percentage of Mexican-American and Black youth. During an interview, the principal of the latter school strongly expresses his prejudices against minority groups and stresses that you impose strict disciplinary measures over these students so as to devote your teaching efforts to "those white pupils who have the capabilities of getting ahead."

What will you do?

Case Study Number 3-24

PRINCIPAL PREJUDICED AGAINST MINORITY GROUP STUDENTS

You are looking for a teaching position for the fall. You are a fairly liberal, open-minded individual and are having an interview with a junior high school principal. Although this fellow has a reputation for being rather conservative, you feel that you could work well under him and you are very favorably impressed with the school itself, the teachers you have met, the department arrangement, and so forth, plus the school has a marvelous heterogeneous group of students. You believe that you would like the job. Then, somehow in the course of conversation, the principal remarks in an offhand manner (with regard to the Black and Mexican-American students): "Well, of course, they haven't the capabilities of our white students so they belong in the home economics and shop classes rather than in the college preparatory classes. We have an obligation to teach them trades."

How will you respond?

Case Study Number 3-25

MINORITY GROUP HISTORY VERY RESTRICTIVE

You are having an interview at a high school in an upper and middle-class neighborhood. The administration and school board discourage the teaching of history which involves the Black's role beyond slavery. Minority groups are not to be distinguished beyond this very restrictive idea.

What would you do?

Case Study Number 3-26

YOUR REACTION TO BEING QUESTIONED ABOUT PERSONAL PREJUDICES IN RELATION TO SECURING A POSITION

You are completing an application for a large city school district which has several schools in a disadvantaged area. It is a well-known fact that many vacancies occur in this particular area each year, and that newly-hired teachers are often used to fill these vacancies. One of the questions on the application asks if you have any prejudices in regard to working with minority children. You have grown up with and *somewhat* accepted the belief that Blacks are intellectually inferior to other races and, therefore, you are not eager to obtain a position teaching them. At the same time, it is very important that you obtain a position in this particular locale since this is where your spouse is employed.

How will you respond to the question?

Case Study Number 3-27

A BLACK SEEKS EMPLOYMENT IN AN ALL-WHITE COMMUNITY

A Black friend of yours has received a letter asking him to interview for a secondary position. Your friend arrived on time, walked over to the office and presented himself to the wide-eyed, openmouthed receptionist who said, “Are you sure you're in the right place?” After standing for fifteen minutes the prospective teacher was asked into the superintendent's office. Your friend was then greeted in a friendly manner by the superintendent who said, “I must say that I was very impressed with your credentials but an indication that you are a Negro would have saved a good deal of embarrassment to you. You see, you are the first person of another race to ever interview for a position at our school and we are not sure of the treatment the community will give you. However, I am willing to hire you if you feel that you can stand the pressure of the community. I think you should have time to think over whether or not you want to keep your application active. Let me know the first of next week how you feel on this matter.” Your friend returns to the university, explains what has happened, and asks for your advice.

What would you say?

Case Study Number 3-28

TAKING PART IN CIVIL RIGHTS DEMONSTRATIONS

You are being interviewed for a teaching position. You are impressed with the community in which the school is located. You appreciate the superintendent's attitude and feel this is the position you have been looking for until he asks, "Are you a member of the National Association for the Advancement of Colored People?" You answer, "Yes." He makes no objection. Then he asks, "Do you intend to take part in demonstrations of the NAACP in our community?"

How would you answer this question?

Case Study Number 3-29

YOUR REACTION WHEN CONFRONTED WITH THE MATTER OF DRAFT RESISTANCE

You are being interviewed for a teaching position. The principal has just stressed the significance of patriotism. You are asked what your attitude as a teacher would be to the question "Are draft resisters good citizens?"

What would your reaction be?

Case Study Number 3-30

YOUR CONSERVATION CLUB CRITICIZED BY SUPERINTENDENT

You have successfully completed the application forms and the preliminary interviews for a teaching position. Indicators have been favorable that you are in a likely position to obtain the job. As the authority for hiring rests with the superintendent, he is the person with whom the crucial interview takes place. It seems to go well until the topic drifts from athletics to the outdoors and conservation. You express your support for the ideals and ideas of the Sierra Club, particularly with reference to the proposed Redwood National Park. The superintendent becomes emotional, excitedly saying that the Sierra Club is just another group of fanatics similar in sort to the nuts of the American Rifle Association who are against any gun control legislation.

How will you respond?

Case Study Number 3-31

YOUR REACTION TO AN INTERVIEWER'S QUESTION AS TO WHAT MAGAZINES YOU SUBSCRIBE TO

You are interviewing for your first teaching position. You have discussed many items that the interviewer wanted to know about you and also you have asked questions about the school system which the interviewer could answer for you. Then he states he has one last question to ask and that is: "What magazine and/or periodicals do you subscribe to?"

What will your reaction be?

Case Study Number 3-32

ASKED ABOUT USE OF ALCOHOL

You are being interviewed for a job as a public school teacher. The principal of the high school is conducting the interview and has mentioned that the community within which the school is located is very conservative and as a consequence subjects teachers to a good deal of scrutiny both in and out of the classroom. He then asks: "You don't drink, do you?"

How will you answer this question?

Case Study Number 3-33

YOUR VIEW ON USE OF DRUGS ASKED

You are a liberal-minded individual. Although you do not use drugs, you feel that the use of drugs is a matter to be explored in class. At a job interview, the interviewer asks you to comment on your view of drugs.

What would you say?

Case Study Number 3-34

ASKED IF YOU ATTEND CHURCH

You are being interviewed for a teaching position. The interview is going well and you are pleased that the principal is favorable to you. During the course of the interview, he asks you about your personal interests. Then he says, "Do you attend church?"

What is your reaction?

Case Study Number 3-35

YOUR REACTION TO A PROPOSITION REGARDING PROPERTY TAXES

You are being interviewed for a teaching position on the staff of a high school. You have been asked about your position on a matter which has been the center of much controversy in the community. It is a measure to increase property taxes in order to raise revenue for the schools.

How would you handle such a question?

Case Study Number 3-36

OPINION OF TEACHERS' STRIKE ASKED

You have just received your credential and are being interviewed for a job. Everything is going fine and then you are asked to give your opinion on a recent teachers' strike in the district.

How do you react?

Case Study Number 3-37

CONFLICT OF POLITICAL VIEWS

You are a prospective teacher, looking for a job. During a preliminary interview with a member of a rather conservative school district, you spend most of the time discussing politics with him. Your views are markedly different than his. At the end of the interview you ask whether he thinks you should submit your application to the district for further consideration. He suggests politely that you should not.

What will your reaction be?

Case Study Number 3-38

INTERVIEW PROBLEM CONCERNING POLITICAL PARTY SPEAKER

In your interview with the assistant superintendent of schools in a very conservative community, he asks, "If the chairman of the Republican Central Committee called and asked if he could come and talk to the students in your class, what would you do? It is an election year."

Case Study Number 3-39

YOUR REACTION TO THE QUESTION, "WHAT ARE YOUR VIEWS ABOUT TEACHING COMMUNISM?"

You are a prospective teacher being interviewed for your first teaching position. The interview is going well until the interviewer says,

"We have recently had some trouble with a pro-Communist teacher and I would like you to give me your views on the teaching of Communism in high school. The inflection of his voice and his facial expression leave no doubt that the man is definitely anti-Communist. You want very much to teach in this particular system, the salary scale is high, and you have many friends within the system, but at the same time you firmly believe in standing up for your views. You believe that Communism should be understood and should be taught objectively but you also believe that saying this will cost you the job.

What do you do?

Case Study Number 3-40

OPINION OF A RADICAL RIGHT-WING GROUP IS SOUGHT

You are being interviewed for a teaching position. The assistant superintendent asks your opinion of a local political group which is commonly viewed as radical right wing.

How will you respond?

RESPONSES TO CASES

Case Study Number 3-1

YOUR REACTION TO A CONTROVERSIAL SUPERINTENDENT

1. Go back to Mr. Jones' office for the interview in hopes of getting the job.
2. Discuss with the assistant principal your unpleasant interview with Mr. Jones.
3. Go to Mr. Jones' office and express your feelings about the job and yourself.
4. Forget the whole thing and go to the next district in search of a position.
5. ______________________________

____

____

Case Study Number 3-2

SUPERINTENDENT NOT THERE FOR INTERVIEW

1. Ask for another appointment.
2. Talk to the secretary.
3. Leave, saying you will call later.
4. THINK TWICE—see if the superintendent is always this way.
5. ______________________________

____

____

Case Study Number 3-3

PRIVATE COLLEGE VS. STATE COLLEGE

1. Tell him you don't like his attitude in choosing a college.
2. Ask him what this has to do with the teaching position for which you are being interviewed.
3. Answer all his questions politely.
4. Try to change the subject back to teaching.
5. ______________________________

____

____

Case Study Number 3-4

YOUR REACTION TO APPARENT IGNORANCE ON THE PART OF THE INTERVIEWER

1. Ignore it.
2. Correct him and see how he reacts.
3. Ignore it during the interview, but keep in mind the man's interest and misinformation.
4. ____________________

____

Case Study Number 3-5

SCHOOL CONSERVATISM

1. Immediately let it be known that you are not the kind of person the school system is looking for.
2. Convince the principal that you have no such ideas of nonsense and are perfect for the job, but later turn down the job if offered.
3. Convince the principal that you have no such ideas of nonsense and try to get hired, worrying about any unpleasant confrontation later.
4. ____________________

____

Case Study Number 3-6

YOUR REACTION TO THE PRINCIPAL'S REMARKS ABOUT FRATERNIZATION WITH WOMEN STUDENTS (Male Teacher)

1. Just keep quiet and hope nothing more will be said.
2. Ask him why.
3. Assure him that naturally you wouldn't even consider it.
4. Inform him that his remark was unjustified.
5. Inform him that his remark was very insulting.
6. Inform him that what you do outside of the class is your own affair, thank you.
7. ____________________

____

Case Study Number 3-7

YOUR VIEW OF DISCIPLINE ASKED

1. Tell the administrator you do not know your position, since you have not as yet taught.

2. Tell him you would prefer handling your own problems.
3. Say: "That's the job of the administrator."
4. Comment that a little physical coercion in the beginning usually stops any further trouble.
5. Suggest that you do not plan on having any discipline problems.
6. Tell the interviewer that you handle the problems as they arise; thus he would have to state a definite example.

7. ____

____

____

Case Study Number 3-8

INTERVIEWER SPENDS MOST OF THE TIME QUESTIONING APPLICANT ABOUT DISCIPLINARY PROCEDURES

1. Go along with some of his ideas on strict discipline in order to look good in the interview.
2. Try to express your own views, in a mild way, so as not to antagonize the interviewer.
3. Strongly argue for your own views hoping to change the interviewer's mind but realizing it may cost you the job.

4. ____

____

____

Case Study Number 3-9

YOUR REACTION TO AN OPPOSING VIEW OF TEACHING

1. Agree with Mr. Jones. Keep silent about your own convictions and consider the position at Maroon High, with the hope that you may be able to apply your own views of teaching.
2. Confront Mr. Jones with your opposing views to see what his reaction will be.
3. Decline the position and look for another school.
4. Agree with Mr. Jones and think about changing your methods to conform to those of Mr. Jones.
5. Tell Mr. Jones what your convictions are but say that you would be willing to conform to the policies of the school.

6. ____

____

____

Case Study Number 3-10

YOUR RESPONSE TO THE ADMINISTRATOR WHO SAYS HE WILL NOT HIRE A TEACHER WHO USES THE NEW APPROACH TO YOUR SUBJECT

1. Tell the principal you would like to use the approach known as the traditional method.
2. Tell the principal that the new method is the only one which should be used.
3. Compromise, tell the principal that you have been trained in the new approach but would be willing to adapt and teach using much of the traditional approach.
4. Tell the principal that although you have been trained in the new method you would be willing to use the traditional approach and exclude altogether the new approach.
5. ______________________________

____

____

Case Study Number 3-11

CONTROVERSY CONCERNING TRACKING OF STUDENTS ON BASIS OF TEST SCORES

1. Let the principal know that you are strongly opposed to only using this particular test and intimate that there are other ways of placing students.
2. Discuss the possibility of setting up local norms based on this particular high school.
3. Say nothing to the principal about your views and hope that you will not be questioned when you place students in classes on some other basis than these particular test scores.
4. Refuse to use this particular test as a basis for placement knowing there is a possibility that you will not be hired because of your views.
5. Attempt to question the principal in order to discover why the school and past counselors have relied so much on one test (e.g., Is it convenient? Is it working or have there been complaints? etc.)
6. Offer alternatives to the concept of "placing," e.g., it is possible to question whether or not "placing" is necessary.
7. ______________________________

____

____

Case Study Number 3-12

INTERVIEW PROBLEM CONCERNING PRESSURE FROM ATHLETE

1. Grade as you always have and plan on looking for another position.
2. Accept the feelings of the community and give Danny at least a "C" grade.
3. Hope for the position you are seeking and let Danny solve his own problem.
4. Let principal make the decision.
5. ______________________________

____

Case Study Number 3-13

QUESTION ABOUT THE UNFAMILIAR

1. Admit that you are not familiar with the subject.
2. Try to lie just enough so that you appear to be vaguely familiar with the subject.
3. Try to switch the subject to something else.
4. ______________________________

____

Case Study Number 3-14

POLICY CONCERNING FEMALE TEACHERS WHO ARE ALSO MOTHERS

1. As position is so perfect, sign contract, and hope your children remain well.
2. Sign contract after deciding that if children are sick you will pretend you are the one who is ill and stay at home with them.
3. Suggest to the principal that you couldn't possibly be the kind of teacher who was sensitive to children's needs if you left your own in their time of need—and attempt to convince him.
4. Tell the principal that your mother lives a short distance away and can stay with your children if and when they are ill.
5. Let the principal know how incensed you are that he should suggest this and, despite your tremendous interest in the position, let him know that it is more important to you to be a good mother than a good employee.
6. Tell the principal that this has created a great dilemma for you as you have a strong feeling of responsibility both for your family and to your profession. Ask him for time to consider and discuss it with

your husband who may be able to take turns with you in staying with the children when they are ill.

7. ______________________________

____

Case Study Number 3-15

LACK OF SPECIFIC TEACHING SCHEDULE

1. Refuse the contract.
2. Try to press the superintendent for a definite promise as to your load.
3. Sign the contract hoping that things will work out the way you'd like.
4. Ask when he may know more and try to wait until then to make a decision.
5. Make a mental list of your priorities trying to decide if scheduling is at the top or bottom of your list.
6. Ask if you can let him know within a week or so, planning to do some additional hunting in the area.
7. ______________________________

____

Case Study Number 3-16

JUNIOR HIGH JOB VS. HIGH SCHOOL JOB

1. Say you don't think you would like teaching at that level.
2. Say that it is just what you like most.
3. Discuss the pros and cons of the position.
4. ______________________________

____

Case Study Number 3-17

TEACHING IN MINOR RATHER THAN MAJOR

1. Accept the position and make the most of it.
2. Explain your lack of training to the principal and accept the position if he still wants you to take it.
3. Accept only if the assignment could be changed.
4. Refuse the position because of lack of training.
5. ______________________________

____

Case Study Number 3-18

ONE CLASS AND FOUR STUDY HALLS

1. Accept the position.
2. Wait until next year for a different opening in that area.
3. Consider a position in a less culturally-advantaged area, hoping to motivate the students to the level of students in the other district.
4. ______________________________

____

____

Case Study Number 3-19

ASKED TO TEACH FAMILY LIFE COURSE

1. Do nothing and make out as best you can.
2. Do nothing now and protest after your appointment.
3. Stop everything and make your views known.
4. Investigate course content more. Then decide.
5. Ask "Does this belong in social studies?" "Or Homemaking?" "Or Physical Education?"
6. Take course and teach what you please.
7. ______________________________

____

____

Case Study Number 3-20

SACRIFICING IDEALS VERSUS A CHOICE AREA FOR TEACHING

1. Accept the first position since it would be more of a challenge to your teaching ability.
2. Accept the second position since the area is a better place to live and the salary is higher.
3. Accept the first position with the intention of teaching only a year or two and then look for a higher paying job.
4. Accept the second position with hopes of gaining some concessions on the part of the principal. Otherwise, leave in a year or two.
5. Accept neither position but rather look for a job which has a high salary in a "nice" area and also a liberal teaching policy.
6. ______________________________

____

Case Study Number 3-21

URBAN GHETTO SCHOOL VERSUS SUBURBAN SCHOOL

1. Take the 7th grade position in the culturally-advantaged neighborhood.
2. Visit the different schools to help you make up your mind.
3. Talk to the principals and enlist their suggestions.
4. Look elsewhere for another job in another district.
5. Look for another job in another field.
6. ______________________________

____

____

Case Study Number 3-22

PRINCIPAL QUESTIONS YOUR ABILITY TO TEACH CHILDREN FROM LOWER SOCIOECONOMIC LEVELS

1. Try to convince him that children from economically secure families can be just as troublesome and difficult to teach as children from low-income families.
2. Assure him that there were a few students in your classes who came from less than desirable family situations. Cite any outstanding or individual problems you faced with these students. Describe your feelings and reactions to these students and your effect on them as their teacher.
3. Tell him you feel that all children, whether from poor or wealthy families, can be reached and motivated through some means. All children have a basic curiosity and interest in life. You feel that you have enough imagination to stimulate this curiosity and interest in any group of children.
4. ______________________________

____

____

Case Study Number 3-23

YOU ARE OFFERED TWO TEACHING POSITIONS AFTER SERVING AS A "VISTA" VOLUNTEER

1. Express your disapproval now so that future confrontations may be kept honest.
2. Remain silent during the interview so as not to endanger your chances of being hired.

3. Forget your interest in the disadvantaged student and accept the more comfortable position.
4. ______________________________

____

____

Case Study Number 3-24

PRINCIPAL PREJUDICED AGAINST MINORITY GROUP STUDENTS

1. Remain silent and keep your feelings to yourself.
2. Ignore the comment and check with other teachers after you have left the interview session. You believe that the principal's stand is very important to your acceptance of a job should it be offered to you.
3. Ask the principal to elaborate on his position. "Oh, then your upper classes are selected on the basis of grades?" Elicit from him without really committing yourself.
4. Interject your feelings—discuss your views with the principal, recognizing that his casual comment may be an interview technique which he is using to get a reaction from you.
5. ______________________________

____

____

Case Study Number 3-25

MINORITY GROUP HISTORY VERY RESTRICTIVE

1. You agree not to teach any more history, than is necessary, about the Blacks.
2. You question the interviewer on this subject, looking for a compromise.
3. You get up and leave without a word.
4. You continue with the rest of the interview but do not intend to apply at this school.
5. You tell the interviewer that Blacks don't deserve to have any history taught about them.
6. You tell the interviewer that he shouldn't be connected with education.
7. ______________________________

____

Case Study Number 3-26

YOUR REACTION TO BEING QUESTIONED ABOUT PERSONAL PREJUDICES IN RELATION TO SECURING A POSITION

1. Indicate your prejudice and risk the possibility of not getting the job.
2. Conceal your prejudice and hope that if you are hired you will be placed in a middle-class school.
3. Conceal your prejudice and accept a position in a Black school with hopes of transferring to a more desirable school at the end of the first year.
4. Indicate your prejudice and try to justify it.
5. Refuse to answer the question.
6. ______________________________

____

Case Study Number 3-27

A BLACK SEEKS EMPLOYMENT IN AN ALL-WHITE COMMUNITY

1. Advise your friend that the community would probably create difficulties which would make his teaching difficult. Advise him to seek an already integrated teaching staff in another school.
2. Advise your friend to be the first to break the racial barrier in the school. Explain that he will make it easier for Black teachers in the future.
3. Discuss the matter, mainly by listening and questioning, without giving your friend any concrete advice.
4. Go to the community with your friend and look the community over more thoroughly.
5. Have your friend contact some of those presently on the school's staff in order to better understand the situation.
6. ______________________________

____

Case Study Number 3-28

TAKING PART IN CIVIL RIGHTS DEMONSTRATIONS

1. You could answer "No" because you have never participated in a demonstration in the past.
2. You should answer "Yes" because of your strong feelings in the matter.
3. Since your job probably will be determined by your answer to this question, and since demonstrations are not expected to occur in this community, it probably would be wisest to say "No."

4. Explain that this is a personal matter and does not in your opinion directly relate to the position you are seeking.

5. ______________________________

____

____

Case Study Number 3-29

YOUR REACTION WHEN CONFRONTED WITH THE MATTER OF DRAFT RESISTANCE

1. Regardless of your personal opinion you answer that democracy is founded on a respect for law.
2. Regardless of your personal opinion you answer that democracy is based on the freedom of dissent.
3. Launch into a discussion of your attitudes toward war.
4. Give a noncommittal answer on the ambiguous nature of the words "citizen" and "citizenship."
5. Answer that this is a matter of personal opinion that should not be dealt with in the classroom.
6. Answer that this is precisely the type of question that would make the notion of citizenship meaningful to students.

7. ______________________________

____

____

Case Study Number 3-30

YOUR CONSERVATION CLUB CRITICIZED BY SUPERINTENDENT

1. Keep your feelings to yourself and be agreeable in order to preserve chances of being hired.
2. Hold your views but agree with the superintendent on special interest points so as to try to find common ground in each other's opinions.
3. Defend your views even at the risk of jeopardizing employment possibilities.

4. ______________________________

____

____

Case Study Number 3-31

YOUR REACTION TO AN INTERVIEWER'S QUESTION AS TO WHAT MAGAZINES YOU SUBSCRIBE TO

1. State to the interviewer that you do not care to discuss this question because it seems irrelevant to the teaching position you are applying for.
2. State your subscriptions.
3. Refuse to discuss the question because it seems to infringe on your private affairs.
4. State that you subscribe to many whether you do or not.
5. ____

____

____

Case Study Number 3-32

ASKED ABOUT USE OF ALCOHOL

1. Tell him the truth, which is that you drink now and then.
2. Lie to him and deny you drink in order to get the job.
3. Tell him you consider the question a little unusual and would rather not answer it at all since it has nothing to do with your educational qualifications.
4. ____

____

Case Study Number 3-33

YOUR VIEW ON USE OF DRUGS ASKED

1. You explain your view of drugs, even though you feel that with this man it is an unpopular one—"Honesty's the best policy."
2. You give him a noncommittal answer that really doesn't say anything.
3. You tell the interviewer that such a question is irrelevant, politely of course.
4. You give him the answer that he wants—anything to get hired.
5. You decide that you would probably not want to teach in this school district anyway; so you excuse yourself.
6. ____

____

Case Study Number 3-34

ASKED IF YOU ATTEND CHURCH

1. Ask the principal what difference it makes.
2. Say that any answer you give would not be relevant to your qualifications as a teacher.
3. Tell him that you go to church regardless of whether or not you do.
4. If you rarely, if ever, attend church tell him precisely that.
5. Be cordial but refuse to sign a contract if it is offered.
6. ______________________________

____

____

Case Study Number 3-35

YOUR REACTION TO A PROPOSITION REGARDING PROPERTY TAXES

1. Refrain from giving a direct answer.
2. Excuse yourself from giving an answer to the question on grounds that you are not familiar with all that the proposition involves.
3. State your case for or against the measure.
4. Agree with what the interviewer has to say about the matter.
5. Suggest to the interviewer in a diplomatic fashion that matters of religion and politics are of private concern.
6. ______________________________

____

____

Case Study Number 3-36

OPINION OF TEACHERS' STRIKE ASKED

1. Evade the question.
2. Make your true views known and hope they are the right ones.
3. Reverse the process and ask for the interviewer's opinion.
4. Confess that your knowledge of the strike is inadequate to make a valid judgment.
5. ______________________________

____

____

Case Study Number 3-37

CONFLICT OF POLITICAL VIEWS

1. Thank him and leave, never submitting the application.
2. Ask him "Why not?"
3. Submit your application anyway.
4. Complain that they weren't interested in you because of political differences, and not because of inability as a teacher.
5. ______________________________

____

____

Case Study Number 3-38

INTERVIEW PROBLEM CONCERNING POLITICAL PARTY SPEAKER

1. Reply that politics have no place in the classroom.
2. Reply that you would allow the chairman to come.
3. Reply that the chairman could come if the school principal consented.
4. Reply that the chairman could come only if representatives of the other parties were also allowed time to talk to the class.
5. Invite representatives from both sides. Proceed even if one side can't come.
6. Have extra curriculum forum.
7. ______________________________

____

____

Case Study Number 3-39

YOUR REACTION TO THE QUESTION, "WHAT ARE YOUR VIEWS ABOUT TEACHING COMMUNISM?"

1. Express your views even though you are ALMOST certain that if you do you will not be hired?
2. Talk around the question in the hopes that the interviewer will decide that you feel as he does?
3. Say what you THINK he wants to hear even though this is not what you believe?
4. ______________________________

____

Case Study Number 3-40

OPINION OF A RADICAL RIGHT-WING GROUP IS SOUGHT

1. Try to figure out with a question or two the position of the interviewer on the right-wing group. Then answer in such a way that he is not offended.
2. Simply say that you haven't given the matter too much thought and are not sure how you feel about that particular group.
3. Say that you don't know what the question has to do with teaching. Say you won't get involved in politics.
4. Give an honest answer as to your feelings about that particular group and let the "chips fall" as they may.
5. ______________________________

____

____

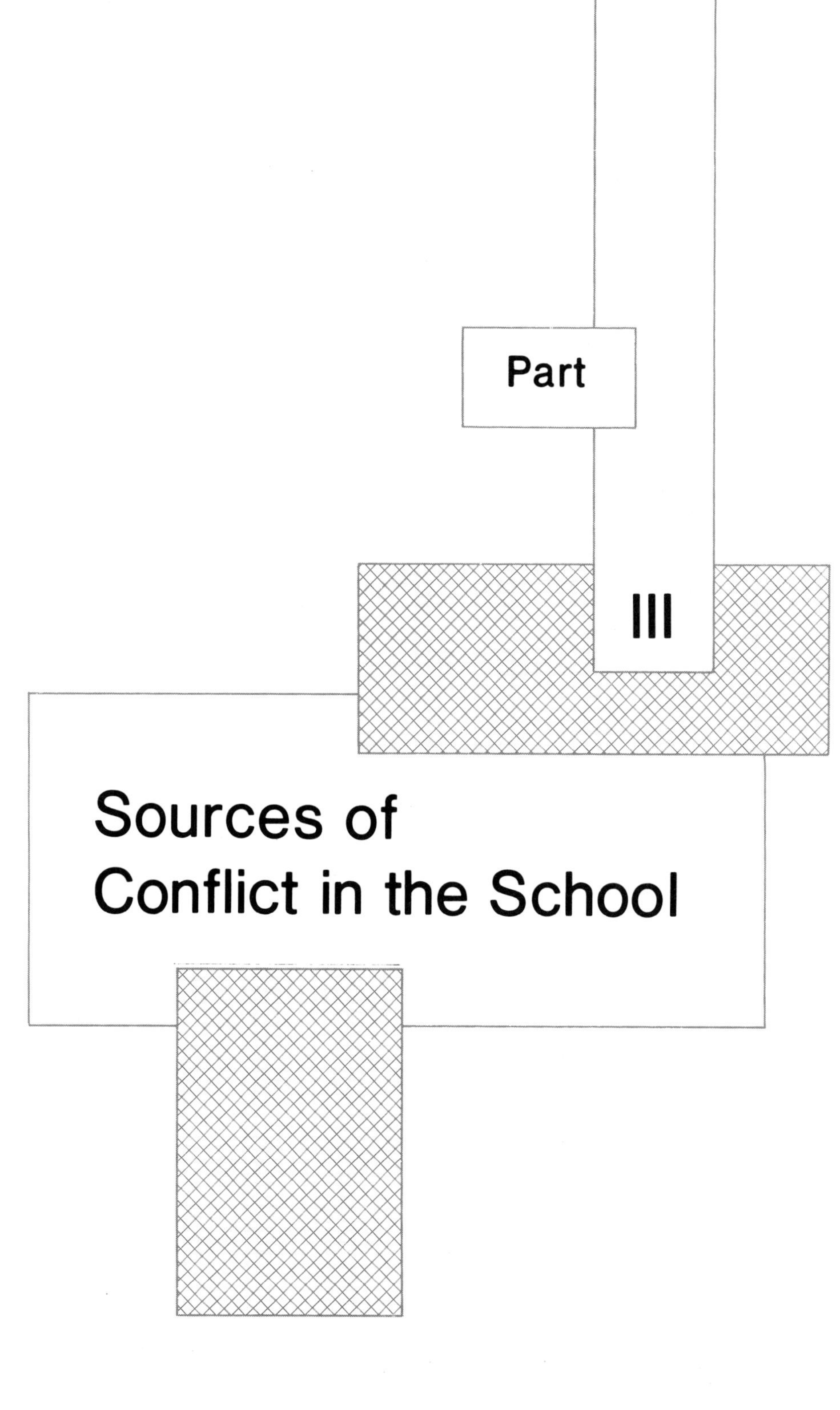

Part III

Sources of Conflict in the School

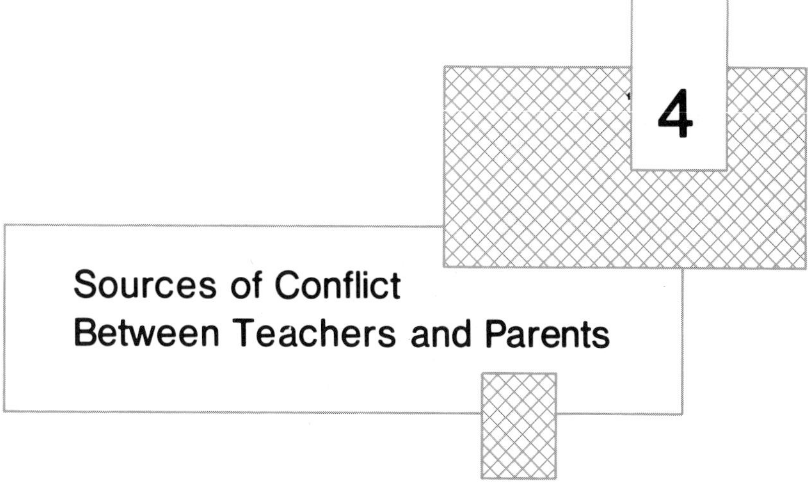

4

Sources of Conflict Between Teachers and Parents

"Sources of conflict" invariably refers to the individuals who perceive conflict to exist. The perception of conflict adds to a conflict situation or creates one where it did not in fact previously exist. In the latter case, for example, a rumor, although completely unfounded, creates tension when known to the party(ies) involved in the rumor. A conflict situation is thus created.

It is then to the perceptions of those involved in the school as a social system that we must turn in order to understand our schools. The study of conflict and conflict situations is consistent with the problem-solving case method employed in this book. Although schools involve more than conflicts, conflict resolution is a part, if not the major part, of the operation of schools.

TEACHERS NOT TRUSTED[1]

Although they are expected to be a model for their students, teachers often feel that parents keep them under extreme surveillance. The result is a double standard, one for the parents and one for the teachers. In some communities teachers are asked not to buy liquor in town, not to drink in places frequented by students, and not to smoke in front of students. Those teachers who smoke retreat to the boiler room in some schools, while parents and board members smoke in the school's administrative offices.

---

[1]Sociologist Willard Waller notes that ". . . the teacher must always be a little disconcerted with the community he lives in. The teacher is a martyr to cultural diffusion." Willard Waller, *The Sociology of Teaching,* John Wiley & Sons, Inc., New York, 1965, p. 40.

It is also difficult for teachers to consider themselves as professionals when they are not trusted to deal with controversial issues in the classroom. Parents appear to be afraid that teachers, especially recent college graduates, will inculcate their ideas in their young people. It is clear, therefore, that parents fear inquiry less than the possible results of such inquiry—that is, student acceptance of foreign ideas.

The lack of freedom many teachers feel adds support to the idea that teachers are baby-sitters. This imposition may cause teachers to transmit a similar kind of surveillance on their students. A double bind is the result.

A final lack of trust in teachers is demonstrated in the adage "Those Who Can Do, Those Who Can't Teach." Parents want the best teachers for their children and yet frequently look down on teaching as an occupation. The bright young teacher is often suspected if he doesn't leave teaching for administration or the university. At the same time, parents are conscious of the importance of formal education in the lives of their children. The public is bombarded with propaganda concerning the dollar and cents value attached to diplomas. Whether or not education is considered to be intrinsically valuable in our society is questionable.

PARENTS HAVE UNREALISTIC EXPECTATIONS FOR THEIR CHILDREN

Some parents expect teachers to discipline their children in a way they are not disciplined at home.[2] The father and mother in many cases both work and give their children money and possessions rather than time. The school is supposed to make up for the loss of many experiences, including discipline. The author remembers being asked to the home of an insolent student. The mother simply could not understand why her son did not study. The boy showed me his room accommodating a television and stereo set. The parents never read anything except the newspaper in their home. The world of the home and the world of the school were entirely different. Yet the parents held the teacher and school accountable for their son's discipline.

Many parents, especially in suburbia, push their children beyond their capacities. Parents want their children to read by the time they are in kindergarten, be loved by the opposite sex at age seven, and begin their higher education at seventeen (in a prestigious university, if possible). One wag has suggested that children be given a B. A. at birth, an M. A. at age two, a Ph. D. at five, and then let the schools get

---

[2]*Ibid.*, pp. 11 & 74.

on with the child's learning. The union card to higher education is a record of good grades. Little wonder that parents pressure teachers for such grades, thus revealing a most important source of conflict between parents and teachers. The student returns home with a poor report card, the parent having to rationalize this in some way. Frequently, the teacher receives the brunt of the criticism. The teacher does not know how to teach, it is claimed, because the student received a poor grade, or the teacher had a personality conflict with the student.

At the same time, it should be added that some parents are disinterested in schools. Such apathy is often the result of their own dislike for school when younger. The result is that the teachers do not feel that they are getting the kind of support they deserve from the parents. The child, in turn, does not receive support at home for his accomplishments at school.

It is difficult for many parents to accept their children's limitations, for these are a reflection of the parents' influence on the child. Yet it is also true that many of the child's limitations are the result, in part, of the school's failures. The student who is decidedly different from the majority of the students is difficult to deal with, for the teacher has all he can do to deal with the majority of the students. Such a student often manifests undesirable behavior patterns. The teacher frequently, then, becomes overwhelmed with specific behavior problems which hinder developing the latent ability of each student. For example, the maturation differences in boys and girls are great at different levels of their school career. Yet, it is difficult for teachers to take this important variable into account, for the teacher often has 150 students a day.

CLASS, RACIAL, AND ETHNIC DIFFERENCES

Consider the following situations: (1) the majority of the teachers in a school are of middle-class origin but the majority of the students are from lower-class homes; and (2) the majority of the teachers in another school are of middle-class origin and the majority of the students are from upper-class homes. In both cases there is a conflict of value systems. In the first case the teacher may be socially advantaged; in the latter case he may be socially disadvantaged. In both cases the teacher would probably be uncomfortable in the homes of his students.

One of the case studies which follows vividly describes the shock of white suburban parents when realizing for the first time that their child has a Black teacher. The Black teacher does not conform to the parents' previously learned stereotypes about teaching and the level of learning reached by Blacks. Racial and ethnic differences between teachers and parents therefore account for conflict between some teachers and parents. In a ghetto school, the white teacher may step out of the role the minority group parent expects him to play, thus creating a basis for conflict.

PARENTS' DOUBLE STANDARD

There is evidence that parents expect the schools to teach their children desirable manners and morals. In most states, these values are supported by law. California law reads as follows: "Each teacher shall endeavor to impress upon the minds of the pupils the principles of morality, truth, justice, patriotism, and a true comprehension of the rights, duties, and dignity of American citizenship, to teach them to avoid idleness, profanity, and falsehood, and to instruct them in manners and morals and the principles of a free government."[3]

At the same time that there is support for prescriptions such as the above, some parents sign letters claiming illness for their children when they "play hookey" or "ditch." Other parents want the schools to train their children to be diligent workers, but do their children's homework. Double standards on the part of parents are an important source of friction between teachers and parents.

PARENTS AFRAID OF INNOVATION

Parents become accustomed to certain behavior on the part of teachers and when this tradition is broken by innovation, parents frequently become anxious. A communication problem and lack of understanding exist. It was discovered in the "new math" projects that parents had to attend their own "new math" classes so that they could understand the nature of this innovation. Social change must always be made legitimate in the minds of parents if the change is to be successful; otherwise parents feel duped by the innovators.

HOMEWORK AND DISCIPLINE

Homework is tangible evidence of student progress. The parents know via homework that *something* academic is going on in the school. Homework is, however, a double-edged sword for the teacher. If parents judge homework to be busywork, or irrelevant, or inappropriate, the teacher is considered incompetent. Homework is also visible evidence of the teacher's desire to discipline the minds of the students.

---

[3]*Education Code,* State of California, Sacramento, Calif., 1963, vol. I, p. 356.

Some parents complain because the school does not discipline their students enough; others complain because the school does discipline the students—usually their child has been punished thus causing the parents to rush to his support. Some parents object to rigid dress standards while others want the school to enforce more rigid standards. The school is damned if it does and damned if it doesn't.

CONCLUSION

Parents and teachers vie for the support of the student. Some parents are threatened because a teacher commands more respect from their child than they do. Part of this is due to hero worship which exists at a certain time in the life of the student, but such respect is also due to the fact that many parents have made significant mistakes in raising their children—mistakes which they cannot easily admit.

Parents often use their children as pawns for their own prestige in the community and with friends. Some parents constantly compare their children to each other and to other children they know. The child who competes favorably usually does not object to this practice; the child who does not often becomes alienated from his parents and the school. The result is discord between the parents and the child's teachers.

Case Study Number 4-1

P. T. A. PRESIDENT WANTS CENSORSHIP

At a PTA meeting the president, a woman, makes a rather vague, nonetheless pointed, comment about the shocking kind of literature available to high school students these days. There is a general mumbling in the room following the president's remark. You know that her son is in a fellow teacher's English class and that the teacher has recently assigned to his students, with department consent, a book written by a Black who makes caustic remarks about "Uncle Toms." The students had previously read *Uncle Tom's Cabin.*

What will your reaction be?

Case Study Number 4-2

CRITICISM FOR DISCUSSING THE "PILL"

During your class, a student offers the idea of the "pill" as being a major socioeconomic difference between the United States and an underdeveloped nation. Without further concentration on that particular subject, the class discussion continued.

That evening one of the students asked her parents to explain the "pill" and its effects on the different countries.

Immediately, the parents confront you, demanding the purpose of teaching birth control in a classroom. Why did you ever initiate such a discussion? Why did you allow such a topic to come up?

What should you do in such a situation?

Case Study Number 4-3

STUDENTS WANT TO DISCUSS CONTROVERSY CONCERNING SEX EDUCATION

The Catholic Women's Guild was flatly opposed. The Mormon Church said, "No." Many parents refused to give their approval also. The issue: Should the local high schools initiate and teach courses in sex education? Hundreds said no. Such information should be taught at home by the parents. It is not a proper subject for the schools to handle. The School Board was in a real quandary. The administrators and teachers were virtually unanimous in their support of the class. A carefully conducted student poll revealed that ninety per cent of the students also favored the addition.

Presently no course in Family and Marriage, Personal Health-Hygiene, or Sex Education was offered. Only a few students acquired such information at school. They were the few who took a physiology course taught by Mr. Perkins; the other physiology instructor, Miss Faurn (a single woman nearing retirement) talked only about the reproduction of flowers and frogs. She seemed too embarrassed to discuss the human animal.

Most students claimed they weren't satisfied with the formal instruction they had received at home. Many found their parents were too shy to discuss such matters. *Dad hemmed and hawed, while mother said* "Talk to your father."

Your students want to discuss the subject of sex education with an eye to how they might act to support their position.

How will you react?

Case Study Number 4-4

CONTROVERSIAL LESSON ON COMMUNISM

You are a teacher who has recently given a controversial lesson on Communism. You get a phone call from an irate parent who feels it is not the function of the school to teach such un-American values.

What would you do?

Case Study Number 4-5

TEACHER CALLED A COMMUNIST

You are a high school teacher and at a community meeting you vocalize strong criticism of our government. The parent of one of your students comes storming into your office calling you a dirty, spineless communist.

How do you react?

Case Study Number 4-6

PARENT ACCUSES YOU OF POLITICAL INDOCTRINATION

You are teaching in a community which is predominantly conservative. It is a presidential election year and you are having a unit on government, politics, and campaigning. You decide to use the presidential candidates as examples so as to relate the unit to the real lives of the students. You aren't campaigning, but are merely pointing out pros and cons of each candidate. An outraged parent gets in touch with you telling you that you are ruining the democratic ideals of your students and you must stop or you will lose your job.

What would you do?

Case Study Number 4-7

PARENT ACCUSES YOU OF BIAS IN TEACHING ABOUT RELIGION

You are covering the period of the Reformation and are using material from outside the text, for example, a film on the life of Martin Luther. The next day you are visited by a Catholic parent of one of your students who vehemently denounces you for bringing in (1) discriminatory material in class, and (2) mixing church and state matters in class.

What is your reaction?

Case Study Number 4-8

PARENT ACCUSES YOU OF TEACHING RELIGION

You are a teacher of world history, teaching at this time the Middle Ages. Mrs. O. comes to school one day irate because Martin, her son, has told her that their religion is a "phony," started only recently by some "rebel" in the Middle Ages. Mrs. O. thinks now that the study of the Reformation and the Church in the Middle Ages should be deleted from the world history curriculum because such study weakens the faith of good people. She says you are teaching religion and distorting it at that.

How would you react to Mrs. O.?

Case Study Number 4-9

YOUR REACTION TO A PARENT WHO OBJECTS TO THE PRESENTATION OF A PLAY

You are involved extra-curricularly with the high school drama group which is about to present *Inherit the Wind,* the play in which the Scopes trial over teaching evolution is presented. An irate parent, a member of a conservative religion, calls you and objects to the play, saying that it's an insult to her faith and to that of many other people. She demands that you don't present it, but choose something else instead.

What will your reaction be?

Case Study Number 4-10

YOUR RESPONSE TO A PARENT'S CRITICISM OF YOUR TEACHING METHOD

In your American Literature class, you bring in records of Bob Dylan and discuss his music as poetry. A parent of one of your students comes to you and protests the waste of his child's time on such "trash."

What will you do?

Case Study Number 4-11

PARENT CRITICIZES YOU IN FRONT OF YOUR CLASS

You are teaching your class one afternoon and a parent knocks on the door. You let her in and she proceeds to criticize your teaching ability by saying that you are not challenging her daughter. This happens in front of all the class.

What would you do?

Case Study Number 4-12

YOUR REACTION TO PARENTS' COMPLAINTS ABOUT TOO MUCH HOMEWORK

You are a member of the social studies department. The parents of one member of your class complain that their daughter in your eleventh grade American History class receives too much homework. They claim that other parents object to the extent of the assignments.

How would you handle this situation?

Case Study Number 4-13

YOUR REACTION TO A PARENT WHO HAS AN AXE TO GRIND ON PTA BACK-TO-SCHOOL NIGHT

You are in your classroom at back-to-school night. There are forty-six parents in your classroom during this third-period class. You have just finished citing the objectives of your course, and made mention of textbooks, equipment, and supplementary materials to be used. You have attempted to answer all general questions and to bring the presentation to a satisfactory conclusion. At this point, just as the period is about to end, a parent seated in the back of the room cries out, "What the hell good is all this junk going to do my kid, anyway?" The bell rings signaling the end of the hour.

What will your reaction be?

Case Study Number 4-14

PRESSURE ON TEACHER BECAUSE OF ABILITY GROUPING

As a teacher in a homogeneously-grouped school, you are assigned the "high" group. The feeling among the parents is that their children are "the cream of the crop." In reality, the progress of some in the class indicates otherwise. Some reasons for this are lack of maturity, indifferent attitudes, lack of ability, inability to function on their own, or overprotection. Instead of assigning grades, you send home class profiles of progress indicating to the parent the child's progress in a period of time and in comparison to the class. The emphasis is on the quality of achievement at the child's own level. One parent sends notes excusing his child's slow work and appears at odd moments during the day to explain his child's tardies, absences, and slow work. Small tokens of kindness flow in for the teacher throughout the year. The parent's one demand is that the child be promoted because his work at home is good and surely he will pick up in school. The mother is in charge of most parent functions. The teacher wonders about the security of the parent's social status. You also wonder who really does the work at home. The child is working under what you feel is undue pressure.

What can you do?

Case Study Number 4-15

PARENTS OBJECT TO CHILD NOT BEING ASKED TO JOIN HONOR SOCIETY

A teacher is serving as the advisor to the Honor Society. Applicants for membership must be screened by all of their teachers as to citizenship, character, leadership, and service. Two applicants were rated rather low and were not invited to join. The parents of one of the disappointed applicants came to school and demanded to know why their child was not admitted to the club.

As the advisor, what would you do?

Case Study Number 4-16

PARENT DOESN'T ACCEPT SON'S LIMITATIONS

You are a ninth grade teacher. The father of one of the students, about whom you have sent home a deficiency notice, comes in to see you about his son, who is earning an "F" in your class. The father, an engineer, is very upset over his son's poor grade and asks to know what he can do to help. He feels the boy isn't studying hard enough and needs to be disciplined. It seems clear to you that the father does not realize his son's limited ability. You explain that the subject is probably too difficult for him, and that he should be in general math. The father seems offended and says, "But my son wants to become an engineer and *must* have the subject!" You refer then to his test scores and point out that he is in the lower decile (10%) on the aptitude test. He discredits the importance of these tests. His son has never done well on them and neither had he, for that matter. This is his only child whom he has raised alone since the boy was three years old, when the mother died, and he feels that he knows what the boy can do.

You want the father to understand the limits of his son's potential, but don't quite know how to help him since he seems to be too emotionally involved to accept the evidence of grades and test scores.

What will you do?

Case Study Number 4-17

A TEACHER'S REACTION TO THE INSISTENCE OF PARENTS THAT THEIR SON IS ABLE TO DO THE WORK OF A GROUP IN A HIGHER TRACK FOR WHICH THE TEACHER HAS NOT RECOMMENDED HIM

You are a member of the college prep department. There are two tracks of your subject and one boy's parents have insisted that he be placed in the first level even though he is receiving a low "B" in the second. The parents have called the principal and he has suggested that you talk to the parents.

What will you recommend to the parents?

Case Study Number 4-18

PARENT OBJECTS TO CHILD'S SPECIAL READING HELP

You have been concerned with a girl in your class who seems to have a high IQ but is far below what you feel she could be doing in reading. You place her in a special group with a reading specialist for two hours a week. A few days later the girl's angry mother comes to the principal saying that her child is very bright and wants her taken immediately out of that class for slow children.

What do you do?

Case Study Number 4-19

YOUR REACTION TO ANGRY PARENT OVER PRIVATE TUTORING OF SON DURING CLASS

You are teaching a relatively advanced class in which a few of your students are slow and cannot keep up with the rest. One boy in particular needs tutoring and you send him to a small room in the rear of the class with a college tutor for 30 minutes of the period three or four days a week. You feel he will learn more this way than to be placed in an easier class. The boy complains to his parents that he is losing friends and being left out; that he is losing prestige with his friends and feels humiliated.

When the parent comes to complain and wants the private tutoring to be discontinued, what will you do?

Case Study Number 4-20

YOU SUGGEST A STUDENT BE SENT TO THE SCHOOL PSYCHOLOGIST. HIS PARENTS ANGRILY REFUSE PERMISSION AND CONFRONT YOU ABOUT THE SUBJECT.

You have a child in your class who has been generally disruptive and disrespectful in class. After hearing similar complaints from his other teachers, you decide to suggest psychological help for him. You tell the administration of your problems with the child and your recommendation that he be sent to the school psychologist. The administration informs the parents and asks their permission for such action.

The parents take great exception to the suggestion and refuse to grant permission. They immediately contact you and demand an explanation for insinuating their child is psychologically unfit.

How do you handle this situation?

Case Study Number 4-21

YOUR REACTION TO AN "UNDER-ACHIEVER"

A rather bright student of yours is constantly tardy, absent, and negligent in his classwork. His parents (he is an only child) are extremely permissive. You have talked with them and they agree that improvement is needed, but nothing happens.

What do you do to awaken them *and* their son?

Case Study Number 4-22

COMMUNICATION PROBLEM WITH PARENTS CONCERNING "RETARDED" STUDENT

You are a teacher. Mary, one of your students, was retained last year. You are watching her progress closely hoping that she will profit by an extra year in the same grade. However, it becomes apparent that Mary is not able to keep up with her class again this year. You feel she needs some special help so you send in a referral on her. Since there are quite a few children on the waiting list you are not surprised when nothing is done immediately, but after several weeks you feel there has been ample time to process her papers. You go to the counselor and ask what conclusions have been reached concerning Mary. She states that Mary does not have average intelligence and therefore she does not qualify for the remedial class. There seems to be no special help for her so you continue to do what you can for her in the classroom. At the end of the year she is promoted to third grade.

After school has been dismissed for the year, the psychologist (without informing you) notified Mary's mother that Mary would be sent to a special school for retarded children. Since you did not have an opportunity to prepare the mother for this, she was shocked. She is unhappy with you, the principal, and all concerned.

What should you do in this situation?

Case Study Number 4-23

YOUR REACTION TO CONFRONTATION WITH PARENT OVER FAILING SON

You are a teacher in an urban area and work with a student body which is 45% Black. You have just issued failing notices to some students in your 12th grade classes. Emil Wilson, a quiet Black student, has received such a notice. One day after school, a modestly dressed woman comes in to speak to you about Emil's failing grade. From her you learn that Emil has no known parents and has been handed down among friends all his life. You learn that he works until one o'clock every night pumping gas to help support his "mother." The woman is irate and tells you that if Emil fails his class, he will not be able to graduate and learn to be a mechanic, a skill in which he has shown much talent.

Your reaction is:

Case Study Number 4-24

YOUR REACTION TO A PARENT WHO REFUSES TO COOPERATE IN HELPING YOU TO WORK WITH HER CHILD

You are a teacher in a disadvantaged area. You have encountered many new problems in terms of the children's behavior, but John, a bright young boy in your class, has some very serious problems. Previous diagnosis and your own observations have led you to the conclusion that he suffers from some form of serious emotional handicap which retards both his academic and his emotional progress. He presents many highly disruptive problems in the classroom daily, and you feel that something must be done. In checking with the school counselor, you find that the emotionally handicapped classes in the district are already overcrowded and there is no hope of having him placed in such a class in the near future. You also discover that the counselor has experienced very little success with this boy in the past, and is a little weary of hearing about him. Determined to find a workable solution, you send a letter to John's mother indicating that you would like to arrange for a conference in the near future in order to discuss John's problems and some possible solutions for them. The next morning you receive the following note from his mother:

> "God made all children different. I realize John is different from other children and he always has been. I have been to school many times to discuss John and I will not come again. We love John the way he is."

What will you do?

Case Study Number 4-25

PARENT WANTS TEACHER TO HELP PRESSURE LOW-ACHIEVING CHILD

You are a teacher. It is near the end of the year and you receive a telephone call from a parent about her low-achieving child. The parent asks what kind of work the child should be made to do during the summer months. You know from parent interviews and from other teachers that the child is very highly pressured to achieve and is very overprotected at home. The child has seemed to make tremendous progress in your class. Your feeling is that if the parent would just relax and ease up on the child, that over the next year things would straighten out on their own.

How will you respond?

Case Study Number 4-26

PARENT OBJECTS TO YOUR GIVING HER CHILD AN F FOR CHEATING

When monitoring a test for another teacher, you are told to take a test away from any student caught talking and give him an automatic "F." This has been standard procedure for the class throughout the year. You catch Johnny talking, remove his paper, and give him an "F."

His mother calls that afternoon after Johnny has gotten home. She has been told a slightly different version of the story by Johnny. She berates you on the phone, saying, "Isn't this cruel, unreasonable punishment for a boy who dearly loves your subject?" She threatens to go to the principal with this. She also accuses you of calling her son a liar.

What will your reaction be?

Case Study Number 4-27

PARENT SAYS YOU ARE CREATING A DROPOUT

You have told Johnny's mother that he is flunking your subject and that he cannot graduate without passing the course. You have tried to motivate Johnny, apparently to no avail. He is doing poorly in other classes but other teachers are giving him a courtesy "D." The mother says that *you* will make Johnny a dropout!

What is your reaction?

Case Study Number 4-28

PARENT ACCUSES YOU OF "PICKING ON" HER SON

You call the parents of John Jones in for a conference. John has been doing poor work, has a poor attitude toward school, but has good ability. His mother comes to the conference and when you state the aforementioned about her son's poor work and attitude, she denies any failing on his part and accuses you of "picking" on him and discriminating against him.

What do you do?

Case Study Number 4-29

PARENT PRESENTS REASONS FOR DAUGHTER'S PROBLEMS

You have sent home a progress report indicating that Barbara Smith is not doing satisfactory work and list suggestions for possible improvement (a normal procedure a few weeks before report cards).

The next day you receive the following letter from Barbara's mother:

"I am well aware of Barbara's talking and concur with all you have said and are trying to do. However, I had a heart attack in January, have had extensive hospitalization since then, and am on very limited activity here at home. Also, Barbara has been ill. She is extremely worried about me and very aware of my health condition. I would prefer that *you* take these things into consideration, too, and not make disparaging remarks about her grades as I don't care to have her feel guilty about not doing well in school. Why don't you people down there at school try to understand some of her problems."

Sincerely yours,
Mrs. A. B. Smith III

What would you do?

Case Study Number 4-30

STUDENT ADJUSTMENT TO NEW SCHOOL

You have a new student in class and he seems to be having quite a bit of trouble adjusting to the change of schools. Although he had always received the best grades in his other school, he is lagging behind in your class. His overanxious parents have become frustrated by his poor marks and thus they come to see you.

What do you tell them?

Case Study Number 4-31

ADMINISTRATOR CHANGES GRADE OF STUDENT

Your school draws students from a fairly wealthy area. These students and their parents are highly college-oriented and there is a great deal of status in the community according to the college or university which one's children attend. Because of the pressure from an angry mother who is quite influential in the community, a student's semester grade has been changed by the administration from a D to a C. You personally feel that the student never put as much into his work as even the average student. His successful subject is Physical Education and he hopes to win some kind of entrance into a "good" college on the basis of his physical abilities. In fact, you as a teacher feel that this student very well earned his D and certainly never deserved the C that some hard-working youngsters from a disadvantaged social class may have struggled to achieve. Not only do you think that this alteration of grade is unfair to the rest of your students but you also feel it is wrong to start this young boy off on the track of believing that he can always get by some way without putting forth real effort.

What are you going to do?

Case Study Number 4-32

INFLUENTIAL PARENT ATTEMPTS TO PERSUADE YOU TO CHANGE HIS SON'S GRADE

You are a teacher in a middle-class suburban high school. You feel that the performance of the students in your class is poor and you give the majority of the class "C," "D," and "F" grades in spite of the fact that the class is considered to be "college preparatory." The father of one of your students, Joe Harmon, to whom you gave a "D" grade for the semester, comes to discuss with you his son's progress and grades in your class. He is very concerned about the low grade which Joe received. He cannot believe that Joe could really deserve to be given such a low grade. He suggests to you that you should be more flexible in your evaluation of the students and that you should change the grade to at least a "C" so that Joe's chances of getting into college will not be ruined. At the end of the conference Mr. Harmon makes it a point to mention that he is an established, influential member of the community, and that he has friends on the Board of Education.

What will your reaction be?

Case Study Number 4-33

YOUR PROFESSIONAL RESPONSIBILITY IN DEALING WITH THE PARENT WHOSE CHILD IS NOT IN YOUR CLASS

You are confronted with a disgruntled parent after school. She wishes to have her son transferred from his present class to yours. She feels his present teacher is unable to discipline him forcefully. You are asked for your impressions of the new teacher and whether you would consider such a move.

How will you respond?

Case Study Number 4-34

PERSONAL PHYSICAL ENCOUNTER WITH A PARENT

You are having a drink with a couple of old army buddies at a local tavern. A man approaches your table, and after introducing himself as the father of one of your students, attempts to start a quarrel. He claims that you unjustly gave his son a "D" in history, and that he doesn't think you are worth a damn, etc. When you stand up to call the bartender over, you notice that the man is considerably intoxicated. He continues his verbal insults and suddenly takes a swing at you landing only a glancing blow on your cheek. The bartender arrives an instant later and the man is escorted from the premises.

What will your reaction be?

Case Study Number 4-35

YOUR REACTION TO THE PROBLEM OF VERY IRATE PARENTS WHO HAVE SOMEWHERE GOTTEN THE IMPRESSION THAT YOU HAVE SEDUCED THEIR DAUGHTER

You are a male teacher with a girl in one of your classes who, you feel, needs special attention outside of class because she does not seem to be understanding the material. You realize she has a crush on you but you don't think too much about it. One day her parents appear in your classroom after school and furiously accuse you of "having relations" with their daughter implying everything in these two words. You know that you have never even spoken to their daughter outside of school or given her the least encouragement, but you assume that they have misunderstood something she has said to them about your tutoring sessions. You would like to get them to understand this before there is trouble.

How do you get them to understand the situation?

Case Study Number 4-36

CONFRONTATION WITH A DISRUPTIVE STUDENT

You are a secondary school teacher. In the process of trying to conduct your class one of your students repeatedly interrupts and takes the class's attention away from you and the subject material being discussed. As a last resort you take him to task for his disruptive behavior and make him look like a complete and utter fool in front of the whole class. That night you get an angry phone call from the parents of this boy who demand to know what right you had to embarrass their child in this manner in front of his classmates.

How do you react?

Case Study Number 4-37

STUDENT PROBABLY BEATEN BY PARENTS

You are a teacher in a fifth grade class in which you suspect that one of the boys is being abused by alcoholic parents although he seems to have an excuse for each bruise or cut. You have met both parents and feel that it may be possible to approach the mother for a conference. Yet, you feel until you are certain about whether there is abuse or not, you can in no way jeopardize what may be the youngster's tenuous position in his family.

What would you do?

Case Study Number 4-38

A PARENT WANTS TO BECOME MORE "CHUMMY" WITH YOU. ASKS YOU TO GO TO A BAR FOR A DRINK.

After the final parent-teacher conference of the day, the last parent, who is of the opposite sex, suggests that you accompany him/her to a local bar for a drink to further discuss his child's progress. The parent wants to get to know you better.

What will you do?

Case Study Number 4-39

PARENT OBJECTS BECAUSE WHITE STUDENT IS IN CLASS WITH MINORITY GROUP STUDENTS

It's open-house night and you are a teacher of a "lower track" class. While you are explaining the class procedures to the other parents, one woman asks, "Why is my son in this class? He does not belong!" An additional complication is that she is white whereas nearly all parents of the other students are Mexican or Black. You don't know who you would offend more, the one white woman or the fifteen "minority" parents.

How would you handle this situation?

Case Study Number 4-40

MEXICAN-AMERICAN PARENT APPLIES PRESSURE ON TEACHER

You are teaching Spanish in high school and the mother of a student whom you flunked recently comes to see you. She cannot understand why her son didn't do well in Spanish since he is Mexican and the whole family uses the language at home. She implies that her son has probably forgotten more Spanish than you (a mere Anglo) will ever learn and demands an explanation for failing somebody in a language he obviously knows.

How do you justify flunking him?

Case Study Number 4-41

PARENT ACCUSES YOU OF PREJUDICE AGAINST CHILD

The parent of your only minority student requests a conference with you. At the beginning of the conference, the mother accuses you of not liking and being prejudiced against her child because the child is a member of a minority group.

What will your reaction be?

Case Study Number 4-42

PREJUDICIAL PARENT CONFRONTS BLACK TEACHER AT OPEN HOUSE

It's open-house night at the school. You are a Black teacher in your first year of teaching. Everything is going smoothly, you meet parents, answer questions like a professional, and feel quite optimistic. Then enters Mrs. Perkins and her daughter Ann. They are both Caucasians. "You are Mrs. Sands, Ann's teacher? Why, Ann didn't say that you were a Negro, but she did say that you were her favorite teacher. I can't understand that. How in the world did you get this job?"

What will your reaction be?

Case Study Number 4-43

A NEW BLACK TEACHER IS REFUSED HOUSING IN THE COMMUNITY

Mr. and Mrs. Shank, ages 80 and 73 respectively, live in a lower middle-class neighborhood in your city. They have five rental apartments which along with their social security provide their income. The neighborhood is primarily Mexican-American together with white Americans. Some Blacks are moving into the outskirts of the neighborhood, but landlords are trying to keep them out.

When prospective tenants look into a vacancy, if they are to her liking, Mrs. Shank will show them the property. If they are not, she tells them the rent is much higher than they can afford to pay, and so they leave.

On occasion groups of prospective tenants visit the neighborhood in organized fashions. A certain group will inquire into the rent of a certain unit and will be quoted a certain price. Later, a second group will inquire and be told either the same price or higher, depending on how they appeal to the landlord. If the tenants are unsuccessful in getting the apartment they want, they will accuse the landlord of race prejudice and threaten to expose them to the authorities. As yet no Negroes have succeeded in moving into the immediate area, but they continue to try.

Recently, a Black was hired to teach social studies in the community. He was refused housing by Mr. and Mrs. Shank.

What is your reaction?

Case Study Number 4-44

THE CITY COUNCIL CLOSES A DRIVE-IN

Sam's Drive-In was on everyone's mind all week. Just about every kid was mad about the City Council's action to close it. Sam's was the only really "in" place in town. It was a real tradition, a landmark. Yet, the city fathers had ordered it closed because it was a "nuisance." Most of the merchants within a block of Sam's, as well as the residents living nearby, had been passing petitions and putting heat on the council for weeks. Complaints, complaints, complaints. "Sam's is noisy—tires squealing, horns blaring, kids yelling 'til all hours of the night"; "Sam's attracts undesirables"; The litter from Sam's covers the whole block—it's the ugliest part of town."

Letters to the editor, complaints to the principal, pressure on Sam, heated and packed council meetings, turmoil within the Chamber of Commerce—all this resulting from the drive-in hassle.

Finally, after weeks of debate, the council moved to close the teen-age hangout. They justified their action with such arguments as "Sam's has been deemed a public nuisance and, therefore, had to be stripped of its privilege to operate as a business in this community."

The town's young population was irate. They claimed Sam's was not a nuisance, that the litter, for instance, was no worse near the drive-in than it was in the heart of town. Charges that the adult community didn't really care about the teenagers and their welfare were rampant among the younger set. "How about all those sleazy bars on Broadway and Miller?" some questioned. "The litter and noise and carousing down there is far worse than anything occurring around Sam's." Some student leaders talked about boycotts, marches, and rallies.

"Youth unite! What about our rights? Can we make the council reconsider its action? Do we have power to do anything?"

As a teacher in the school system what will your reaction be to your students' request for support? Will the type of students requesting support influence your decision?

RESPONSES TO CASES

Case Study Number 4-1
P. T. A. PRESIDENT WANTS CENSORSHIP

1. Keep your feelings to yourself and hope that the whole topic will be dropped.
2. Talk with the English teacher (who is not present) and tell him of the comment and unrest at the meeting. Express your views to him.
3. Discuss the matter of assigning "questionable" literature at a department meeting.
4. Discuss the matter with the school administrators—be sure of their position. Will they back you or side with the parents?
5. Discuss the matter with your students in your English classes.
6. Confront the PTA president individually.
7. Stand up in the PTA meeting and express your views.
8. ______________________________

____

____

Case Study Number 4-2
CRITICISM FOR DISCUSSING THE "PILL"

1. Tell the parents you are not a mind reader; how could you have supposed such a statement would have come up.
2. Say a mistake was made but it will never happen again.
3. Explain to the parents the purpose of discussing socioeconomic background of countries. Explain further that it was not to give an education in birth control, but the student's answer did have relevance.
4. Tell the parents to get used to the idea of birth control and the "pill"; it is a part of our country's history.
5. Tell the parent that you will run the class the way you feel is best; if they do not like it then remove their child.
6. Bring the subject up in class the next day, to find out whether they feel the "pill" really does affect the economy of a country.
7. Bring the subject up again in class; ask the children if the parents were right or not.
8. ______________________________

____

____

Case Study Number 4-3

STUDENTS WANT TO DISCUSS CONTROVERSY CONCERNING SEX EDUCATION

1. Refuse to allow your class to become a forum for the discussion of sex education.
2. Invite people with different viewpoints from the community to express their views to the students in your social studies class.
3. Point out to your students that they can discuss the matter in class but as the teacher you will not support any action on the basis of this discussion.
4. Introduce your students to the political machinery they can use to effectively realize the power they have.
5. Ask groups opposed to sex education in the schools for time at their next meeting in order to present your point of view on the matter.
6. ____

____

Case Study Number 4-4

CONTROVERSIAL LESSON ON COMMUNISM

1. Defend your position adamantly.
2. Give in to the parent.
3. Compromise your position with that of the parent.
4. Put the parent on the defensive.
5. Invite the parent to come and sit in on the class so that he can judge for himself whether the lesson is un-American.
6. ____

____

Case Study Number 4-5

TEACHER CALLED A COMMUNIST

1. Apologize saying that you got a bit carried away and that it will not happen again.
2. Refuse to talk to him.
3. Get mad at him but say as little as possible.
4. Get mad at him and tell him that he is a narrow-minded ignoramus.
5. Try to calm him down and defend yourself rationally.
6. ____

____

Case Study Number 4-6

PARENT ACCUSES YOU OF POLITICAL INDOCTRINATION

1. End the unit.
2. Continue and take the consequences.
3. Try to convince the parent why you are teaching the unit, and why you think it is valuable to the students.
4. Take the matter up at a PTA meeting.
5. Ask the principal for his opinion.
6. Quit your job.
7. ____
   ____
   ____

Case Study Number 4-7

PARENT ACCUSES YOU OF BIAS IN TEACHING ABOUT RELIGION

1. Show her the lesson plan for the following week which has a film on the Counter Reformation and point out things presented in class on an "equal time" basis.
2. Point out that the material is partially covered in the history text which is state approved and that you are merely fulfilling your role in informatively "teaching history."
3. Ask her to sit in on class if she likes, to see for herself if there is undue bias in the teaching presentation and/or "warping of the facts."
4. Ask her to talk to her priest and get his opinion of the incident (church point of view) in hopes that he will convince her that your approach to the subject was justified and proper.
5. ____
   ____
   ____

Case Study Number 4-8

PARENT ACCUSES YOU OF TEACHING RELIGION

1. Tell her that tomorrow you will spend the day telling the class how important the Reformation was and how good the Protestant churches were for that period. Also promise to work on deleting that period from the curriculum.
2. Tell Mrs. O. you will go over that section with Martin again because he obviously got the wrong idea.

3. Invite Mrs. O. to come and talk to the class about the Reformation.
4. Smile at Mrs. O. and nod your head occasionally, fully intending to go on doing what you have been doing.
5. ____

____

____

Case Study Number 4-9

YOUR REACTION TO A PARENT WHO OBJECTS TO THE PRESENTATION OF A PLAY

1. Hang up on him.
2. Try to explain evolution.
3. Get into a religious argument with him.
4. Tell him that free speech is guaranteed in the United States and the fact that he has a right to shout against evolution, your student actors likewise have the equal right to speak in favor of it.
5. Agree with him, and try to get the play changed.
6. Tell him that you're sorry he's offended, but too much time and effort and money have already been spent to change it now.
7. ____

____

Case Study Number 4-10

YOUR RESPONSE TO A PARENT'S CRITICISM OF YOUR TEACHING METHOD

1. Apologize and say that you will not do it again.
2. Outraged, defend Dylan as a poet.
3. Explain to the parent your educational reasons for teaching Dylan: gaining the students' interest, involvement, and enthusiasm which can then be directed to the more traditional poetry.
4. Show the parent the results of your teaching method (improved achievement on tests and papers).
5. Ask him to sit in on the class and see the effect himself.
6. Maintain that you are the teacher and a parent has no right to question your methods.
7. ____

____

Case Study Number 4-11

PARENT CRITICIZES YOU IN FRONT OF YOUR CLASS

1. Try and calm her down and usher her out of the room.
2. Go next door and ask a fellow teacher to take your class so that you can talk to the parent.
3. Talk right back to the parent explaining that she has no place in the classroom unless she has cleared this with the principal and yourself.
4. Call the principal and let him handle this case.
5. Discuss the case with your students after the parent has left so that you maintain your relationship with the students.
6. ______________________________

____

____

Case Study Number 4-12

YOUR REACTION TO PARENTS' COMPLAINTS ABOUT TOO MUCH HOMEWORK

1. Ignore their suggestions to reduce homework assignments because you think the work is justifiable.
2. Change the nature of home assignments and eliminate so-called "busywork."
3. Ask students the length of time they spend on homework.
4. Ascertain whether students spend so much time on homework because of its length or difficulty.
5. Discuss with teachers in other departments the extent of their assignments in order that students have sufficient time to deal with all subjects adequately.
6. ______________________________

____

____

Case Study Number 4-13

YOUR REACTION TO A PARENT WHO HAS AN AXE TO GRIND ON PTA BACK-TO-SCHOOL NIGHT

1. Pretend you didn't hear him and hope he leaves.
2. Try to give him a brief but hopefully clear answer to his question.

3. Ask him to remain after the others have left and try to give him a clear answer to his question.
4. Ask him his name and make an appointment for a later date.
5. Ignore the question and ask your principal's advice at a later time.
6. ______________________________

____

____

Case Study Number 4-14

PRESSURE ON TEACHER BECAUSE OF ABILITY GROUPING

1. Educate the parent in the methods of reporting progress.
2. Tell the parent that the child is doing fine work for his level.
3. Threaten to retain the child if his work doesn't improve.
4. Offer to spend time with the child for special help.
5. Ask the parent to reinforce school work at home without threatening.
6. Discuss the problem with the principal.
7. Be quiet and allow time to take its course.
8. Praise the child for his class work when he shows improvement.
9. Accept the child in spite of the conflict with the parents.
10. Take your feelings toward the parents out on the child.
11. ______________________________

____

____

Case Study Number 4-15

PARENTS OBJECT TO CHILD NOT BEING ASKED TO JOIN HONOR SOCIETY

1. Tell the parents to go see the teachers who rated the child so low.
2. Tell the parents the information is confidential and cannot be given out.
3. Tell the parents the child was not the only one rated low.
4. Tell the parents exactly where their child was rated low but do not mention the teachers who did it.
5. Tell the parents the child was generally rated low.
6. Tell the parents the school will reconsider and accept the student.
7. ______________________________

____

____

Case Study Number 4-16

PARENT DOESN'T ACCEPT SON'S LIMITATIONS

1. Refer him to the counselor who is better equipped to explain the test scores to him.
2. Let the student continue in the course, but inform the counselor of the apparent discrepancy between his ability and and aspirations.
3. Take the boy aside and talk to him about the possibility of other fields of work where math is not so heavily stressed.
4. Discuss with the counselor possible courses of action.
5. ______________________________

____

____

Case Study Number 4-17

A TEACHER'S REACTION TO THE INSISTENCE OF PARENTS THAT THEIR SON IS ABLE TO DO THE WORK OF A GROUP IN A HIGHER TRACK FOR WHICH THE TEACHER HAS NOT RECOMMENDED HIM

1. Give in to the parents and recommend the boy for the higher track so that the parents can recognize the boy's ability for themselves.
2. Try to reason with the parents persuading them to leave the boy in the second track and letting them compare his work to the work expected of those in the first track. The teacher would then bring out work done by the boy and some papers of the students in the higher level.
3. Compromise—let the parents send the boy to summer school with the agreement that if he does well he can be placed in a higher track.
4. ______________________________

____

____

Case Study Number 4-18

PARENT OBJECTS TO CHILD'S SPECIAL READING HELP

1. You can show the mother proof that her daughter is obviously reading below her ability and tell her that the special class will help her.
2. You explain that you also feel that the girl is very bright and that this class will help her improve her reading since it is not for "slow" children, but for children with special problems.

3. Knowing that the mother is a real problem, you try to stay away from her and let the office take care of the situation.
4. You immediately take advantage of this situation to find out if there are any problems at home that might be causing her reading problem.
5. ______________________________

____

____

Case Study Number 4-19

YOUR REACTION TO ANGRY PARENT OVER PRIVATE TUTORING OF SON DURING CLASS

1. Explain his need for private tutoring, trying to convince the parent to agree, and refuse to discontinue the tutoring.
2. Agree to discontinue the private tutoring and to put him back with the class, although you know he will probably fail.
3. Suggest to the parent that he talk with the principal about possibly placing the boy in a different class.
4. Agree to put him back with the class and spend extra time yourself tutoring him after school.
5. ______________________________

____

____

Case Study Number 4-20

YOU SUGGEST A STUDENT BE SENT TO THE SCHOOL PSYCHOLOGIST. HIS PARENTS ANGRILY REFUSE PERMISSION AND CONFRONT YOU ABOUT THE SUBJECT.

1. You tell the parents you feel they are at fault for the child's discipline problems. Generally, a child's conduct reflects the training he has received at home.
2. You refuse to meet with the parents to discuss the problem.
3. Meet with the parents and assure them that their child is not mentally disturbed. Tell them you do feel, however, that his conduct problem could be improved by talking with the school psychologist. Try to persuade them that the child could benefit by such a meeting.
4. ______________________________

____

____

Case Study Number 4-21

YOUR REACTION TO AN "UNDER-ACHIEVER"

1. Fail him, despite potential.
2. Get principal to threaten non-graduation.
3. Recommend counseling help.
4. Make special last effort to deal with student individually.
5. Transfer student to another teacher's class as there may be a personality conflict between you and the student.
6. ______________________________

____

____

Case Study Number 4-22

COMMUNICATION PROBLEM WITH PARENTS CONCERNING "RETARDED" STUDENT

1. Uphold the mother because you realize this matter has not been handled wisely. The mother should have been warned of the possibility of this happening several months ago. A second reason for your decision is the fact that you personally feel that Mary will learn more in a regular classroom.
2. Uphold the school even though you feel they made a mistake in waiting until school was closed to inform this mother.
3. Since you weren't consulted or informed as to what was being done, you could refuse to be involved at this time.
4. ______________________________

____

____

Case Study Number 4-23

YOUR REACTION TO CONFRONTATION WITH PARENT OVER FAILING SON

1. You offer to give Emil extra help and extra assignments so that he may pick up his grades.
2. You refer her request to the principal, leaving the decision in his hands.
3. You will try to be more understanding to Emil's difficult situation when it comes to marking his next quiz.

4. You adhere to school policy which states that a student must have at least a D grade in all required subjects to graduate. Thus, this assures that Emil will fail to graduate for he would have to score B on his remaining test to pass.
5. ____

____

____

Case Study Number 4-24

YOUR REACTION TO A PARENT WHO REFUSES TO COOPERATE IN HELPING YOU TO WORK WITH HER CHILD

1. Contact John's parents again and hope to convince them of your sincerity in wanting to help.
2. Turn to your guidance counselor who has long since given up on the case.
3. Consult with your principal.
4. Isolate John from the rest of the class to at least spare them from his continual interruptions.
5. Work very closely with John at school and do your best to come to a solution.
6. Ignore John on the basis that if everyone else is not concerned, why should you bother.
7. ____

____

____

Case Study Number 4-25

PARENT WANTS TEACHER TO HELP PRESSURE LOW-ACHIEVING CHILD

1. Tell the parent what you think and that she should get off the child's back and leave her alone.
2. Put the parent off about specific work but encourage a teacher-parent conference to discuss the situation.
3. Put the parent off by saying you will send assignments and information with the child but you have no intention of doing so.
4. Tell the child about the call but say she should not worry because you aren't going to send any assignments home.
5. ____

____

Case Study Number 4-26

PARENT OBJECTS TO YOUR GIVING HER CHILD AN F FOR CHEATING

1. Caught off guard you become upset and second the motion—in anger—that she take it to the principal.
2. You become defensive and say that that's "the way it is."
3. You keep calm and explain your side after she has finished talking. You tell her that Johnny knew the rules beforehand and that it was his responsibility to live up to them.
4. You give in to her because you really didn't agree with the other teacher's policy anyway—besides you were only doing a favor. You suggest that she also talk to the teacher of that class.
5. Try to reason with the lady and then after the phone call is over go to the principal and acquaint him with the facts of the case.
6. ______________________________

____

____

Case Study Number 4-27

PARENT SAYS YOU ARE CREATING A DROPOUT

1. Discuss the problem frankly with the parent in Johnny's presence. Leave the grade as is.
2. Discuss the result of #1 with the principal.
3. If Johnny cannot do better, change the grade to a "D."
4. See if a good student in the class would like to tutor Johnny.
5. Take Johnny's parents to the staff room and over a cup of coffee with other of Johnny's teachers present discuss his lack of motivation in all his classes. This would serve to point out the possibility that Johnny's parents need to take more interest in Johnny.
6. ______________________________

____

____

Case Study Number 4-28

PARENT ACCUSES YOU OF "PICKING ON" HER SON

1. Drop everything connected with this case.
2. Contradict her and show her mistakes.
3. Invite parent into classroom for a few days.
4. Get consensus of other teachers.
5. Get cumulative files. Have content in mind.

6. Call in counselor for meeting with parent.
7. Call in principal for meeting with parent.
8. Ask mother for evidence.
9. ____

____

Case Study Number 4-29

PARENT PRESENTS REASONS FOR DAUGHTER'S PROBLEMS

1. Take it as all in a day's work.
2. Present it to your principal and ask his advice.
3. Send a letter home telling her to show you a little consideration for having feelings and intelligence.
4. Take the girl aside and really give her a talking.
5. Talk to the previous teacher and ask about her relationship with the home.
6. Call the mother immediately and get things settled.
7. Write a letter home expressing your intentions in regard to Barbara's progress and your interest in her mother's health, apologize for the misunderstanding, and request a conference at the family's convenience. Notify principal of action.
8. ____

____

Case Study Number 4-30

STUDENT ADJUSTMENT TO NEW SCHOOL

1. They expect too much too soon—they should let the boy alone.
2. His former school wasn't as advanced as the new one—perhaps he should be kept back a year.
3. He needs special attention in certain areas.
4. His grades are due to the new environment and he should improve with time.
5. ____

____

Case Study Number 4-31

ADMINISTRATOR CHANGES GRADE OF STUDENT

1. Call the student into conference and try to work through his value system with him. Help him to see what he is counting important and some of the ramifications of his actions.

2. Have a series of discussions in your class on the meanings and values of education and of each other's value systems. Have students present reports, panel discussions, post composition, etc. In other words, get all the students in your class really thinking and analyzing their values.
3. Talk with the parents of the boy, perhaps with the school counselor present, and try to help them see the ramifications of what they are doing.
4. Really stick your neck out and give luncheon speeches to community groups about the values of a real education and the contrasting superficiality apparent in the community.
5. ____________________

____

____

Case Study Number 4-32

INFLUENTIAL PARENT ATTEMPTS TO PERSUADE YOU TO CHANGE HIS SON'S GRADE

1. Overlook the incident and give the boy the "D" grade.
2. Try to help the boy by giving him special help outside of class.
3. Report the incident to the principal (to tell your side of the story before Joe's father talks to him) but do not change the grade.
4. Change the grade to a "C."
5. ____________________

____

Case Study Number 4-33

YOUR PROFESSIONAL RESPONSIBILITY IN DEALING WITH THE PARENT WHOSE CHILD IS NOT IN YOUR CLASS

1. Frankly and confidentially discuss the difficulties facing the new teacher.
2. Explain that her son must learn to adjust to unfavorable situations.
3. Decide that you would be violating professional standards to allow the discussion, suggesting instead a conference with the principal.
4. Call the office and ask for the principal to come to your classroom as soon as possible.
5. Suggest that she make an appointment to discuss the matter with the other teacher.
6. ____________________

____

Case Study Number 4-34

PERSONAL PHYSICAL ENCOUNTER WITH A PARENT

1. Shake off the whole matter without further action, attributing the man's behavior to his intoxicated state.
2. Report the matter the next day to the principal and ask him what should be done about it.
3. Ask that the boy be transferred to another class as quickly as possible.
4. Arrange for a meeting with the boy and see if he desires to remain in your class and, if so, offer assistance toward his getting a better grade.
5. Ask for a conference to include the principal, the father and the boy, and yourself to discuss the matter.
6. Report the matter to the police bringing assault charges against the father.
7. ____

Case Study Number 4-35

YOUR REACTION TO THE PROBLEM OF VERY IRATE PARENTS WHO HAVE SOMEWHERE GOTTEN THE IMPRESSION THAT YOU HAVE SEDUCED THEIR DAUGHTER

1. You try to calm them down and look at the situation rationally.
2. You get angry and argue with them on their own emotional level.
3. You refuse to discuss the problem until both a school administrator and the daughter are present.
4. You refuse to discuss it at all hoping that the parents will become more reasonable after a good night's sleep.
5. You hand the entire matter over to a school administrator to handle.
6. ____

Case Study Number 4-36

CONFRONTATION WITH A DISRUPTIVE STUDENT

1. Refuse to answer any questions.
2. Tell them to make an appointment with you through the school secretary at which time you will discuss the matter.

3. Try to tell your side of the story over the phone and why you felt that this type of discipline was the best for all concerned.
4. Tell them to take their gripes to the principal.
5. Apologize and say that it will not happen again.
6. ____

____

____

Case Study Number 4-37

STUDENT PROBABLY BEATEN BY PARENTS

1. Refer the youngster to the school nurse after having informed her of your suspicions and let her handle the matter.
2. Refer the youngster (in the same manner as #1) to the school counselor or psychologist.
3. Bring the matter of your suspicions to the attention of the principal.
4. Wait and see if you can ascertain abuse.
5. Have a conference with the mother based on the pretext of discussing school progress and casually mention that her son certainly seems to be "accident prone."
6. Invent an excuse for a conference with both parents and have literature from Alcoholics Anonymous conspicuously displayed on your desk.
7. Express your concern about the youngster to the mother and hope that you can gain her confidence so that she will be able to see that there is a problem.
8. Request a conference with the mother, express your concern over the well-being of the youngster and ask that he be seen by the family physician if there is one. (If not, then suggest the school physician.) Have the mother sign an "exchange of information" form so that you may communicate your concern to the family physician.
9. ____

____

Case Study Number 4-38

A PARENT WANTS TO BECOME MORE "CHUMMY" WITH YOU. ASKS YOU TO GO TO A BAR FOR A DRINK.

1. You thank the parent but say you have more work to do.
2. You gladly accept the invitation.
3. You accept the invitation but suggest that you go to a coffee shop instead of a bar.

4. Since the child involved is doing better than average work you tell the parent that you are unable to accept the offer because of other duties.
5. You tell the parent that if he wants to talk further about the student you will schedule another conference.
6. ____

____

____

Case Study Number 4-39

PARENT OBJECTS BECAUSE WHITE STUDENT IS IN CLASS WITH MINORITY GROUP STUDENTS

1. Tell her to see the principal, this is not your concern.
2. Tell her that the son is not performing well and so has been placed in your class.
3. Tell her to meet with you afterward—something can be arranged.
4. Tell her that the son might have been programmed in the group because of lack of space in other classes.
5. Tell her that this is an ethnically mixed school and she should not complain because there is no way to avoid the situation.
6. Tell her that this class is meant for those kids who do not put forth any effort, and the main cause for this lies in the home.
7. Tell her to see the principal and that her son can easily be moved out of the class.
8. Tell her that the son does not belong and you will see that he is changed to a different class.
9. ____

____

____

Case Study Number 4-40

MEXICAN-AMERICAN PARENT APPLIES PRESSURE ON TEACHER

1. You go to great length to point out that, though her son does indeed speak Spanish, he was graded on his ability to read and write the language and on his attitude and attendance, all of which were poor.
2. You do not elaborate on the reasons why he was flunked but rather pass the buck by suggesting she see the counselor and attendance office staff in order to get a better idea of her son's problems in reading, writing, failure to attend school regularly, etc.

3. You suggest that she attend some P.T.A. meetings and by doing so acquaint herself with the criteria teachers use when grading students. You further suggest that if she disagrees with what she finds out she ought to work within that group for some sort of change in grading and other areas that may concern her.

4. ______________________________

____

Case Study Number 4-41

PARENT ACCUSES YOU OF PREJUDICE AGAINST CHILD

1. Claim you are not prejudiced.
2. Admit we're all human and that you have some prejudices.
3. Tell her that she's the one who is prejudiced.
4. Determine why she thinks you are prejudiced.
5. Mention all the occasions when you are not prejudiced (especially against her child).
6. Ask the child to join the conference.

7. ______________________________

____

Case Study Number 4-42

PREJUDICIAL PARENT CONFRONTS BLACK TEACHER AT OPEN HOUSE

1. Smile and move on to the next parent.
2. Ask Mrs. Perkins what difference race means as long as the person is qualified for a position.
3. Become angry, let Mrs. Perkins know where you stand, letting the chips fall as they may.
4. Ask other teachers about Mrs. Perkins at your next opportunity.
5. Ignore the matter as much as possible. Forget it knowing that Mrs. Perkins is simply another bigot.

6. ______________________________

____

Case Study Number 4-43

A NEW BLACK TEACHER IS REFUSED HOUSING IN THE COMMUNITY

1. Owners of property have the right to choose their own renters. Ignore the matter.

2. Although you know that Mr. and Mrs. Shank are wrong, nothing can probably be done about this matter and so try to smooth it over.
3. Take this matter to the City Council for action.
4. Discuss this matter informally with your colleagues and then act.
5. Take this matter to the next faculty meeting.
6. Take this matter to your teachers' organization.
7. Discuss this matter in your social studies classes.
8. Discuss this matter in your classes and then devise a plan of action. Help your students organize picket lines around the Shank home if this is what the students decide to do.
9. Discuss this matter with administrators in your school.
10. Rent the apartment yourself and then sublet it to the Black teacher.
11. Take this matter to the City Council of Churches.
12. ____________________

____

Case Study Number 4-44

THE CITY COUNCIL CLOSES A DRIVE-IN

1. Refuse the students' request for a point of view. Stay out of the argument altogether.
2. Discuss the matter in your classes but do not endorse a particular point of view as you are the teacher.
3. Discuss the matter in your classes and endorse a particular point of view.
4. Personally appear in front of the City Council to express your views.
5. Send a letter to the editor of the local newspaper in order to have your position known.
6. Take the matter to the next teachers' meeting for discussion.
7. Take the matter to your teachers' organization for discussion.
8. ____________________

____

____

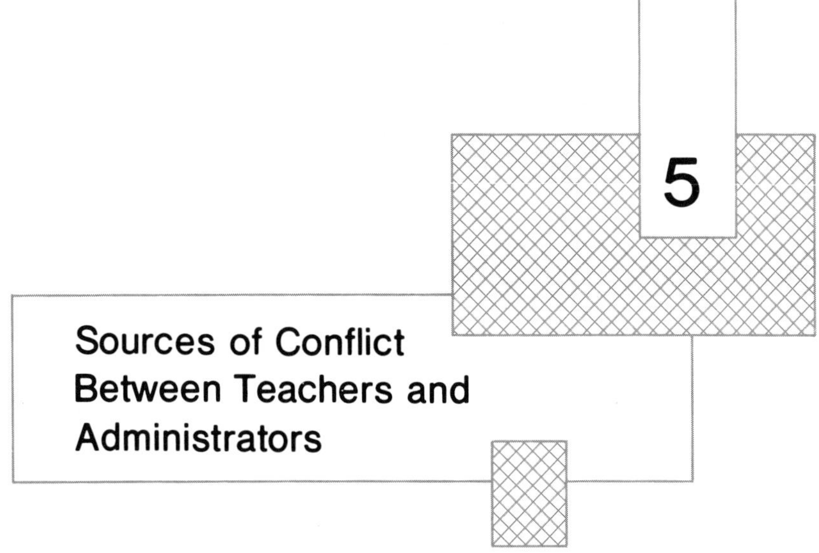

5

Sources of Conflict Between Teachers and Administrators

Administrators are usually former teachers who have changed roles. It is common knowledge that promising young teachers frequently look to administrative positions as a part of their career pattern. The community at large and other members of the school as a social system also anticipate such mobility. Failure to recognize important differences in the roles of teachers and administrators as well as incompetent people often playing administrative roles is the source of conflict between teachers and administrators.

ADMINISTRATORS TOO SENSITIVE TO THE PUBLIC

Part of the folklore of the teaching profession is the story of the principal reprimanding the teacher because of one parent's phone call. Teachers often feel that administrators are much too sensitive to the public. Administrators in turn talk about the naivete of teachers in not recognizing the influence of the public on the schools. Without at least the tacit support of the public, administrators are in peril of losing their jobs. When a new administration enters a school system there is a honeymoon period, but as soon as the new administration starts making decisions which influence the children of the school, some parents will be angry thus crying for the dismissal of the newly formed administration. Although principals act in part as buffers of criticism aimed at teachers, some teachers make serious mistakes—mistakes which often come to the immediate attention of the principal through a single phone call. In such cases the teacher must be checked for the welfare of his students.

Teachers, claiming that administrators are public relations men rather than educational leaders, criticize administrators for impeding progress by stifling innovation. The administrator who wants to innovate needs support.

TOO MUCH BUSYWORK

Teachers, like their students and some administrators, complain about the excessive amount of busywork or petty tasks they are required to perform. Teachers are frequently asked to collect lunch money, supervise the cafeteria, sell accident insurance to the students, and fill out a multitude of forms throughout the day. The school, in order to protect itself from public criticism, requires evidence in writing at nearly every step of the educational process. The results of this are evident in the commonly heard remark that teachers are baby-sitters.

Related to this issue is the matter of the incongruous roles teachers are often expected to play. The teacher is supposed to be a scholar, teacher, and policeman. The watchdog role frequently expected of teachers is demonstrated to an extreme degree by the principal who suggested that male teachers crawl up into trees at the rear of the campus in order to take pictures of smokers. In this way there would be clear-cut evidence of rule violation.

Teachers often feel that administrators do not understand the academic role teachers are expected to play, since administrators are not scholars but primarily public relations men. Teachers frequently see themselves as political pawns for administrators who are out for their own personal gain.

In short, many teachers feel that our schools are obsessed with trivia at the expense of the major goal our schools should have—that is, the creation of an atmosphere in which students learn. Classroom interruptions, in the form of suddenly called assemblies, public address announcements, and taking students from class for class pictures make teachers antagonistic toward administrators.

DISCIPLINE

Going to school is compulsory; teacher-student ratios are high; and philosophies on discipline are multifarious. These help account not only for the existence of discipline problems but also for their perpetuation. It is little wonder, then, that discipline is a source of irritation between administrators and teachers. Both are subjected to criticism by the other on this issue: some are considered too easy on the students; others are considered drill masters; and still others are considered out of touch with modern learning theory. Teachers frequently complain that administrators do not support them in discipline matters, while principals complain that teachers are not skilled in handling behavior problems.

A behavior problem that provokes disciplinary action by the teacher which is challenged outside of the school often brings tension into the teacher-administrator relationship. Administrators usually give vocal support to their teachers prior to such incidents. However, they appear to support the superintendent and board of education rather than teachers after a conflict situation arises. This, among other reasons, is why teachers feel administrators engage in duplicity, thus creating a gap between administrative rhetoric and reality. The fact that most administrators are former teachers explains in part the role conflict which many administrators feel in dealing with teachers.

There is a sense in which the principal cannot win with his teachers: teachers want to feel a closeness with the principal and yet feel threatened when such closeness occurs because of the power the principal has over teachers. Teachers claim administrators are not available to teachers and yet the same teachers complain of "snooping" when they feel the administrators are spending too much time around their classrooms or in the teachers' lounge.

The administration has a great deal of power over teachers thus accounting for much of the anxiety teachers feel when confronted by administrators. The administration controls the budget, sanctions materials used by teachers, offers or fails to offer tenure to new teachers, assigns classes to teachers, and generally runs the school. The teacher who wants to get his pet project funded naturally promotes such a project to the exclusion of other important matters. The administration cannot afford such a narrow view on budgetary matters.

Yet, it is certainly true that there are many different administrative styles. Some principals coerce their teachers to join the National Education Association (for unlike the American Federation of Teachers, administrators are allowed to become members of the N. E. A.) and give their fair share to the charitable causes they support. Other principals refuse to employ such coercive methods. Some principals play favorites with teachers—for example, in giving their friends the best classes to teach. Others are not accused of such favoritism.

All of these problems and more are the subject of the following case studies which deal with conflict between teachers and administrators.

Case Study Number 5-1

YOUR REACTION TO A PERSONALITY CONFLICT WITH YOUR PRINCIPAL

You've been teaching in the same school for several years under the same principal, with whom you feel a slight personality conflict. In addition, you are beginning to feel that your professional qualities are being overlooked (i.e., you get no praise for a job well done, you are not recommended for special workshops you apply for, etc.).

What would you do to remedy the situation?

Case Study Number 5-2

AGREEMENT WITH UNPOPULAR PRINCIPAL THREATENS RELATIONS WITH STAFF MEMBERS

You are chairman of your department in a secondary school. The principal is not well liked but has some very good ideas for the school. You often agree with these new ideas. Because of your status, personality, and dynamic teaching qualities, you are influential with staff and administration.

At a committee chairmen meeting between administration and staff, you observe that the other department heads are aligned against the principal's new proposal. You agree with it. Your vote and opinion are respected. However, the atmosphere is tense and you risk losing a lot of potential cooperation from the staff if you go along with the principal.

What will you do?

Case Study Number 5-3

PRINCIPAL ASKS YOU TO DEMONSTRATE GOOD TEACHING FOR FELLOW TEACHER

You are a member of a secondary school's staff. You have taught in this school for two years; therefore, do not have tenure. Another teacher, Mr. X., is new in the school and teaches the same subject and grade level as you do. He has been having extreme difficulty in organizing his lessons. These difficulties do not seem to concern Mr. X, but the principal is very concerned. The principal calls you in and asks, "Would you consider taking over Mr. X's classes for a week while he observes you? I'll give you a couple of days to think it over."

What will your reaction be?

Case Study Number 5-4

NEW TEACHER OPPOSES ADMINISTRATORS AND TEACHERS

Mr. Lucken, a middle-aged principal, is extremely well liked by most of his staff. Working relations for the most part are excellent.

A new teacher arrives in mid-year and the scene changes. She appears to make the last half of the year miserable in every way she can, especially for Mr. Lucken. The new Miss Thorp gossips and makes snide remarks about the staff and community relations, etc. The original staff cannot tolerate her actions.

How can this clash be remedied?

Case Study Number 5-5

ADMINISTRATOR PRESSURES NEW TEACHER TO JOIN TEACHER ORGANIZATION

You are a first-year teacher and your administrative superior also happens to be the building representative for the combined local-state-national educational associations. He personally encourages you to join these associations. However, you have not decided whether to join the education associations or the local teacher's union. When you mention this, he says that the union members are just troublemakers and that you should stay away from them for your own good. When you don't immediately join, he makes a plea at faculty meeting for 100% membership in the education associations. Since you are the only new teacher and the school has apparently had 100% membership in the past, the point of his remarks is not lost to anyone.

How will you respond?

Case Study Number 5-6

TEACHER SEEKING TENURE IS ASKED TO STRIKE

You are a teacher in a suburban school and are presently up for tenure now that it is near the end of the year. Your local teachers' union has called for a teachers' strike to protest the poor teaching facilities and low pay given teachers. Your administrator has made it very clear that anyone participating in the strike will jeopardize his teaching position.

What will your reaction be?

Case Study Number 5-7

PROMISE TO TEACH ONLY IN YOUR MAJOR UNFULFILLED

You are presently teaching three classes in your major and one in your minor. The administrator in charge previously inferred when you were accepted for the position that you would eventually have only those classes in your major to teach during your second year of teaching. At the end of the first year you are assigned two classes in your major and two in your minor.

What would you do?

Case Study Number 5-8

YOUR REACTION WHEN YOUR PRINCIPAL BREAKS HIS PROMISE AND GIVES A LONG COVETED POSITION TO SOMEONE ELSE

You are a secondary school teacher. You have long wanted to head the Honor Club. The principal has assured you that if this position ever opened up, it would be yours. Instead he gives it to another teacher.

What will your reaction be?

Case Study Number 5-9

YOUR REACTION WHEN CONFRONTED WITH ANOTHER IN A LONG LIST OF EXTRA-CURRICULAR ASSIGNMENTS

The principal has just announced to the faculty that the Honor Club, for some reason or another, is not permitted by the district to staff the kitchen for the pancake breakfast with four faculty supervisors. Instead, each member of the faculty is about to draw kitchen detail. You had made arrangements to be in another city over the weekend, and have just found yourself assigned to the 6:30 to 8:30 A.M. pancake cooking brigade for Sunday morning.

What will your reaction be?

Case Study Number 5-10

EXPERIENCING TOO MUCH WORK AND TOO MUCH PRESSURE, YOU ARE ASKING FOR A REDUCTION IN YOUR WORKLOAD AND A REVISION OF YOUR WORK SCHEDULE

You are a new teacher in a school. You take over in its entirety the former teacher's workload and schedule. After teaching a few months, you find the workload too heavy and the schedule excessively demanding. You seek relief through the administration.

The administration desiring a certain amount of time to be spent on the subject looks disapprovingly at your demand. They question why you are unable to handle the schedule as it had been arranged for the former teacher. Are you simply trying to get out of work? Do you really enjoy teaching? Why don't you accept the status quo?

How do you handle this situation?

Case Study Number 5-11

YOU DISAGREE WITH RECOMMENDED BOOK LIST

As with all new teachers, the principal calls you into his office for a conference to review the list of recommended books for your classes. You notice that the list does not offer the student a wide range of views.

What will your reaction be?

Case Study Number 5-12

CHOOSING TEXTS

You are a secondary teacher. The year has come to get a new text series for your school. After examining a number of companies' samples, talking to various representatives of the companies, and conferring with other professionals, you decide on what you feel to be the outstanding series. Your administrator gives the "okay" to place your order on requisition sheets. At the next school board meeting an influential member speaks to the administrator concerning a series he happened to see and thought was very good. Your superior returns, strongly suggesting that you take a "second look" at X series to see if perhaps it may be better.

What will your reaction be?

Case Study Number 5-13

BUDGET CUT IN YOUR AREA

You are a second year art teacher and you have been asked to make out a supply list for your classes for the following year. You have been allotted a particular sum of money which will only barely meet what you feel to be the minimum needs of your students. After you have made out your list, cutting all possible corners and your list has been approved by the department chairman, you learn that the administration has decided to cut the department budget in half.

What should you do?

Case Study Number 5-14

YOUR REACTION TO A PRINCIPAL WHO DOES NOT CARRY THROUGH WITH AN ACTION HE HAS INDICATED HE WOULD COMPLETE

You are teaching in a particular school district for the first time. Prior to the opening of school, you have spent several days attending a district orientation workshop in order to become familiar with the materials that will be available to you in this district. Upon arriving at your assigned school, you begin to gather some of these materials for use in your classroom. You soon discover that the majority of these materials are missing from the central storage area of your school and you are unable to find any record that they have been checked out. You ask your principal where the materials can be found and he responds that many of the teachers keep these materials in their rooms rather than returning them to the central location. He assures you, however, that he will obtain the materials you have requested.

School begins and you have not yet received the requested materials. After a few days you approach the principal again and indicate that these materials are important to your program. He appears annoyed at having been reminded of this problem but promises to take care of it. Several weeks pass but nothing more is done about your situation.

What will you do?

Case Study Number 5-15

PREJUDICE AGAINST LOW ACHIEVERS

A new teacher finds that his class is comprised of low achieving, low I.Q. children. His classroom is poorly lighted and the heating system doesn't work at all. He discovers that although there aren't enough texts to go around and materials are scanty, the other two fourth-grade classes are adequately provided for in all areas. He eventually concludes that the principal has decided not to "waste" resources on lost causes. The children are so fully discriminated against that only a "green" teacher can be spared to teach them.

The teacher disagrees with the practice of the administration he is working under and decides to "buck the system" in whatever constructive way he can. He confronts the principal with a list of grievances and requests action upon them. He is given, however, the run-a-round: "More supplies will soon be ordered", "When?" "Oh, within the next few weeks." The lights and heating system are to be attended to in the immediate future. Only months go by and nothing is improved and all of the same unfair conditions prevail.

How can a teacher in this situation make his feelings known to the principal and persuade him to improve the lot of the children?

Case Study Number 5-16

ADMINISTRATOR OBSERVES YOUR CLASS

At each appearance of an observing administrator, you feel the class becomes very stoical. Yet the administrator praises you highly for your work. But this is not your regular routine; the class as well as yourself change immensely when being observed.

You wonder whether you should be teaching the way you do when you are observed since you have been so highly acclaimed.

What should you do?

Case Study Number 5-17

YOUR REACTION TO THE ADMINISTRATOR'S CRITICISM OF YOUR TEACHING METHODS IN THE CLASSROOM

You are a teacher who has not yet received tenure at the junior high school where you are teaching. Each year it is required that you be evaluated by the principal during the course of the year. Your approach is highly unorthodox in respect to traditional ideas of classroom control and objectives. Your students work at their own speed on different projects. There is the appearance of chaos and disorder in the room because the students are free to wander around the classroom and talk with the others. The principal makes it known that he does not approve of your manner of handling the class. He shows his disfavor by criticizing you in front of your class.

What will your reaction be?

Case Study Number 5-18

YOUR DECISION ON HOW BEST TO TEACH STUDENTS WHO WILL NOT LEARN IN THE TRADITIONAL WAY

You are an experienced teacher in a new school. It is the principal's policy to make three observations of your class during the year. Having three classes of very difficult youngsters, you decide to innovate and stray from the established curriculum; the class decides to write plays, journals, short stories, etc. about life as they see it. Your administrator feels that the curriculum must reflect order and discipline and sees this activity as a waste of time.

What will you do?

Case Study Number 5-19

HANDLING OF CONTROVERSIAL ISSUES IN CLASS

You have been teaching at the high school level for several years. At regular intervals during the year you devote some periods of your civics class to a discussion of controversial issues related to student experience in some way. During these discussions you attempt to see that all sides of an issue are presented. The principal tells you to avoid bringing such controversial matters into the classroom because they can create unpleasant situations.

What would be your reply to the principal's suggestion?

Case Study Number 5-20

PARENT SAYS YOU'RE TEACHING CREEPING SOCIALISM

A student in your class, whose father is head of a radical conservative group, has been continuously objecting to the way you teach. He has claimed that your teaching is merely another manifestation of creeping socialism. He has objected to your authority on the grounds that you've never been out in life and done anything, ending by proclaiming "Those who can, do; those who can't, teach!"

What will your reaction be?

Case Study Number 5-21

PRINCIPAL ASKS YOU TO STOP GIVING OPINIONS IN CLASS

You have been presenting your opinions in class, usually when asked by the students; they have been presented as your opinion only. The principal receives a phone call and asks you to stop, for the sake of objectivity.

What do you do?

Case Study Number 5-22

DISCUSSION OF SEX IN CLASS

As a tenth grade teacher you have been discussing the problem of overpopulation as it pertained to Japan, China, and India. The students became very interested as the discussion turned to causes of overpopulation and what some areas had tried in order to limit births—contraceptives, abortion, etc. The discussion was open and frank, and many of the students wanted more information. How do contraceptives work? Why are abortions illegal in the United States? Some of the students were concerned with the problems discussed and wanted to talk more to their parents about these matters.

A few of the parents became quite upset at the questions that were asked of them. They wanted to know where they had gotten all of these ideas. When they learned that they had been discussed so openly in school, several of them became incensed and called on the principal of the school. As he was new on the job and wishing to please the community (several of the complaining parents were very influential in town), he calls you into his office and warns you that if you do not stop talking about such controversial topics in class you will have to leave the district.

How will you respond?

Case Study Number 5-23

STUDENT ACTIVISM VERSUS PRINCIPAL

Your classes want to have a "sit-in" during lunch in the cafeteria because they want to discuss (perhaps harangue) a current social problem with other students. They feel that they should use current social methods to bring the problem to the attention of the other kids. The principal says definitely not!

What is your reaction?

Case Study Number 5-24

ROLE CONFLICT: POLICEMAN OR TEACHER?

Because of a recent water balloon fight at the bus loading zone, you have been assigned to bus loading duty three weeks out of the school year. In addition to this you must also take your turn in supervising detention after school—a privilege which becomes yours about twice a month. Besides this you must also uphold many other specific rules around the school, such as hall passes for students in the hall during class time and many similar restrictions that all the teachers are required to enforce. You feel that the punitive image these responsibilities develop is highly detrimental to your relationship to the students. Your own philosophy is that an instructor should be a friend and a counselor as well as a teacher, and you really feel hampered by this situation.

What should you do?

Case Study Number 5-25

YOUR REACTION UPON BEING CRITICIZED BY AN ADMINISTRATOR FOR ACTING AGAINST SCHOOL POLICY

As a high school teacher you have been assigned the task of looking for students smoking on campus. The school procedure has been that if a student is caught smoking he is to be reported immediately to the principal or other administrator. On your patrol duty you catch a student who is in one of your classes and whom you personally like a great deal. You are at odds with the administration's disciplinary tactics and feel that you personally can handle the problem better, so you do not report the student. Somehow the incident is made known to the administrator in charge of such matters and he criticizes you for not reporting the incident as is demanded by school policy.

What stand are you going to take?

Case Study Number 5-26

SMOKING AND POSSESSION OF TOBACCO ON SCHOOL GROUNDS

Mrs. Jones, Dean of Girls of Centerville High School, suspected certain girls of possessing cigarettes, but she was unable to prove her suspicions. Two girl informants gave her the names of girls whom they saw smoking in the rest room.

Mrs. Jones, also a P. E. teacher, decided to search the girls' purses while they were busy with P. E. activities. The purses were left in the valuables' room. Mrs. Jones found cigarettes in several purses which she took to the Dean's office for the girls to identify.

The girls, excepting one named Ann, confessed to possessing cigarettes. Ann denied having them for her own use, claiming that she was holding them for another person.

Ann's parents came to school and objected violently to Mrs. Jones' searching the purses and her subsequent decisions. Her parents are very wealthy and very influential in the community. The other parents did not visit the school, nor did they complain or question the actions of Mrs. Jones.

The other girls were suspended for one week, and Ann was placed on probation for three days. Probation means the student stays in school, but is not permitted to participate in school activities.

You are a teacher in the school. What is your reaction to this situation?

Case Study Number 5-27

ENFORCEMENT OF DRESS CODE

Your high school principal has decreed that T-shirts are underwear and should be worn only under a shirt. The exception to this ruling is that some shirts which look like T-shirts actually are not because they have pockets and/or a collar. Therefore, such shirts which look like

T-shirts, but have pockets or collars, are acceptable dress for male students. You are a teacher in this high school and in the Monday morning homeroom period (first period) following the issuing of the "new" dress regulations, nine of the fourteen young men in your class are wearing white T-shirts with varicolored pockets sewn on (no one attempted a collar) with colorful thread or yarn. As far as you can see, the pockets are functional and all nine of the wearers are smiling confidently. In the course of taking roll you realize from the students' talk that other homeroom teachers are faced with about the same array of T-shirts with patch pockets.

How will you respond?

Case Study Number 5-28

YOUR HANDLING OF THE PRINCIPAL'S REQUEST THAT YOU TELL YOUR CLASSES THAT YOU DIDN'T REALLY MEAN WHAT YOU SAID ABOUT MARIJUANA

You have been discussing marijuana in your class, and you say that although you wouldn't advise anyone to smoke marijuana, you do feel that the current laws restricting its use are overly strict. One of your students feels that this is a sanction to smoke marijuana and goes home and tells his parents that Mr. _____ was all for smoking this drug. The parents call the principal and complain and he, in turn, calls you in and asks you to retract your statements about marijuana in front of the class, and tell them that the drug is bad in all situations and that its use should be strictly prohibited. You feel that you cannot do this because it would undermine your authority with the class, and because you feel that it is wrong to make a public statement that you do not and cannot believe in.

What should you do?

Case Study Number 5-29

PRINCIPAL QUESTIONS YOU ON DISCIPLINE PROBLEMS

You are teaching when the telephone rings. The school secretary asks you to come to the office to see the principal. The principal says that he is busy at the moment but would like to see you between classes. You return to your class and then see the principal.

"Mr. Smith," the principal says to you, "I wanted to talk to you about Jack Soldron, the boy you kicked out of class yesterday and sent to the office. I have his side of the story and now I would like to hear your side of the story."

"Well as you know," you begin, "I've had a problem with Soldron all year. He's a real problem. I've had it up to here with him, so I sent him in to you yesterday hoping that he would be disciplined."

"Well, Mr. Smith," the principal says, "it's not just Soldron that you have had problems with all year—how about the Knox boy, the Blotz girl, and several others?"

How will you respond?

Case Study Number 5-30

DISAGREEMENT OVER DISCIPLINE

Whenever you send a student to the vice-principal for disciplinary reasons, the student returns with a note reprimanding you without the problem having been treated. You lose control over these students who like to create trouble because nothing has been done to change their behavior. The students are friends of the vice-principal. Order and control start to break down.

What do you do?

Case Study Number 5-31

YOUR RESPONSE TO AN ADMINISTRATOR'S COMPLAINT OR CHARGE OF YOUR LACK OF CLASS CONTROL

You are a teacher with rather liberal teaching techniques. Class participation of students usually ends in very boisterous enthusiastic student discussions and arguments which annoy the teacher next door. Your class appears uncontrolled although it is actually academically stimulating to the students. The principal calls you in and suggests that you change your classroom techniques.

How will you respond?

Case Study Number 5-32

PRINCIPAL VISITS CLASS FREQUENTLY THUS DISRUPTING YOUR CLASS

It is your first year of teaching in a school with an enrollment of 1200 students. The principal likes to be on a first name relationship with his teachers and staff and promotes a relaxed atmosphere. He frequently visits your class, two or three times a week, and asks questions of you about the topic of discussion, using your first name in front of the class. He also frequently cracks jokes for the benefit of the class.

What will your reaction be?

Case Study Number 5-33

ADMINISTRATOR'S HOAX—A BOMB SCARE

On a recent fall morning the students arriving at Centerville High School were surprised to be met at the parking lots by Mr. Sands, high school principal, and police officers. Students were informed that they were not to enter the buildings but to go directly to the football bleachers. They were told that this action was necessary because of a bomb threat to the school.

Students responded cooperatively. Investigation continued for several hours but no bomb was found. Students were then directed to report to their classes. Many students were frightened and most disturbed. No one thought the "joke" was very funny.

Then, at noon, more than a year later, Mr. Anderson, director of student activities, announced on the intercom that another bomb threat had been phoned in to the school. He directed all students to report immediately to the bleachers. Once again fear mingled with disgust was shared by all the students. Once all the students were seated on the bleachers and all was quiet, the cheerleaders came onto the field to conduct a pep rally for the next football game. The bomb threat was all a hoax to get the students together.

You are a teacher in this school? How would you react?

Case Study Number 5-34

CONTROVERSY OVER TEACHERS' MEETING

You're very disturbed by the insignificant issues discussed at a recent faculty meeting. You feel the really important matters were left unsolved and a lot of time was wasted on petty matters. You feel this should not continue.

What do you do?

Case Study Number 5-35

AN ADMINISTRATOR ASKS TEACHERS FOR HELP ON THE SCHOOL BOND ISSUE

The high school principal was most interested in demonstrating to his superiors that he was behind their efforts to pass a school bond election. The principal, therefore, asked his teachers to do everything possible to support the passing of the issues at hand. Some teachers argued that teachers are professionals and therefore should not take part in this kind of political issue. They argued that the teacher should be somewhat detached from the students and their parents. They said that teachers are not interested in the mechanics of getting money and therefore the administration should take care of this matter. Another group of teachers felt that the teachers should take an active part in this matter and even go from door to door to sell the people on the school bond matter. You are a teacher in the school.

What would you do?

Case Study Number 5-36

THE PRINCIPAL GIVES NEW TEACHERS ADVICE ON BUYING LIQUOR IN TOWN

Each year the principal has an orientation meeting for new teachers. At this meeting he asked the teachers not to buy liquor in the suburban town (10,000 people) where the school was located. He said that this did not look good and some students would probably see you. As the teacher you should set the example for the students.

What is your reaction?

Case Study Number 5-37

BEER SERVED AT TEACHERS' MEETING IN YOUR HOME

You are teaching in a small town. You suggest that one of the teachers' evening meetings be held at your home "for a more relaxed atmosphere." Refreshments are served at your home of which beer is included. Several days later the principal calls you in the office and tells you that several parents have called complaining that a teachers' meeting is no place to be drinking—what kind of an example are the teachers to the children?

What do you do?

Case Study Number 5-38

COMMUNITY CENSORSHIP

You are a tenth grade teacher in a small conservative town. You want to take your class to see the play "The Country Wife." A few parents of the students started complaining that this was not a play for their children to see. The school board took action and asked to see you about this. They told you not to take the class to see the play. You felt that it was worthwhile for your class to see it.

What will your reaction be to the school board?

Case Study Number 5-39

PRINCIPAL REACTS TO YOUR DATING A STUDENT

You have been teaching in a particular school for about 10 years and have established good rapport with both the administration and faculty. You are satisfied with the position in all aspects. You are a bachelor and have likewise established a social life outside the school. Among your friends is a family whom you have grown close to due to church and political connections. This year their daughter is enrolled in your class. She is bright and a hard working student and is doing "A" work. Suddenly you find that you have a great deal in common and you begin dating. The relationship is discovered by members of the class who are complaining that your "girl friend" is being graded unfairly. It is brought to the principal's attention via the parents of the other students. He asks you in light of preserving the dignity of the school and his position in teaching to stop dating the girl.

What would your reaction be?

Case Study Number 5-40

PRINCIPAL THREATENS FIRING UNLESS YOU LOSE WEIGHT

As a part-time physical education teacher you have become a great deal overweight. The school principal calls you in and explains that unless there is a loss of weight you will not be rehired as a physical education teacher because you serve as a poor example of what you teach.

If you were the teacher, what would you do?

Case Study Number 5-41

YOUR REACTION TO AN IRATE ADMINISTRATOR UPON YOUR RESIGNATION

You have had a most successful year of teaching. Your administrator has contributed greatly by giving counsel and support to your ideas and innovations. He has even expressed his appreciation of your merits to other colleagues and wishes to promote you to the position of department chairman for the next academic year. On the basis of your reputation as a master teacher you are offered a better and more rewarding teaching position in another school district for the next year. You deliberate for a reasonable length of time and then accept the new job offer. After informing your administrator of your decision he becomes furious. He berates and belittles you both privately and publicly. He makes it obvious that the remainder of the school year will be unpleasant if you do not reconsider and remain at your present teaching position.

What will your reaction be?

RESPONSES TO CASES

Case Study Number 5-1

YOUR REACTION TO A PERSONALITY CONFLICT WITH YOUR PRINCIPAL

1. Talk to other teachers about your feelings.
2. Talk to the principal about your feelings.
3. Plan to look for another position.
4. ______________________________

____

Case Study Number 5-2

AGREEMENT WITH UNPOPULAR PRINCIPAL THREATENS RELATIONS WITH STAFF MEMBERS

1. Stick by what you believe in and agree with the proposal.
2. At the meeting try and bring the other members around to seeing beyond their personal opinions of the man and to the practicality of his proposal.
3. Agree with your fellow teachers on this so that you won't lose their cooperation in the future when you need it.
4. Refuse to take a stand on the matter and let the principal fight his own battles.
5. Inform the principal beforehand, tactfully, that he is losing the cooperation of his staff and that he faces some real opposition.
6. ______________________________

____

Case Study Number 5-3

PRINCIPAL ASKS YOU TO DEMONSTRATE GOOD TEACHING FOR FELLOW TEACHER

1. Take over Mr. X's classes to comply with the principal's wishes.
2. Refuse and risk your good standing with the principal.
3. Tell Mr. X he's in trouble and offer to help him.
4. Have Mr. X come to your class to observe if he wishes.
5. ______________________________

____

____

Case Study Number 5-4

NEW TEACHER OPPOSES ADMINISTRATORS AND TEACHERS

1. The principal may suggest exchanging positions with another teacher in another school in the district.
2. Accept the fact that she is young with no teaching experience and perhaps she will improve by the end of the term.
3. Suggest that she learn to control her tongue and become more professional by imitating a more successful staff member who is in good standing throughout the school district.
4. Urge the principal to ask for her resignation.
5. ____

____

____

Case Study Number 5-5

ADMINISTRATOR PRESSURES NEW TEACHER TO JOIN TEACHER ORGANIZATION

1. Join the local-state-national organizations to avoid conflict with the administrator.
2. Join the teachers' union and ask for protection from the administrator.
3. Do not join any organization but contact teachers' union about administrative pressure.
4. Do not join any organization and hope to maintain a neutral position.
5. See the superintendent and register a complaint about pressure from the administrator.
6. ____

____

____

Case Study Number 5-6

TEACHER SEEKING TENURE IS ASKED TO STRIKE

1. Although sympathetic to the cause of the teachers as represented in the strike, you do not participate because of your own welfare and that of your family.
2. Join the strike and make your views known.
3. Make yourself absent from school the day of the strike with an illness excuse. Return to school a few days later hoping that the conflict will have died down.

4. Use the strike as a topic for conversation in your classes.
5. Go to the principal and ask him for more explicit advice.
6. ______________________________

____

Case Study Number 5-7

PROMISE TO TEACH ONLY IN YOUR MAJOR UNFULFILLED

1. Accept the assignment without saying anything to the administrator.
2. Accept the assignment but let the administrator know you are disappointed.
3. Do not accept the assignment until you have expressed your views to the administrator.
4. Do not accept the assignment. Ask the administrator for what was promised. If you don't receive it, look for another job.
5. Leave the system for another job.
6. ______________________________

____

Case Study Number 5-8

YOUR REACTION WHEN YOUR PRINCIPAL BREAKS HIS PROMISE AND GIVES A LONG COVETED POSITION TO SOMEONE ELSE

1. Get furious but just keep to yourself.
2. Complain about it to several of the teachers in your in-group.
3. March right into the principal's office and demand an explanation.
4. Proceed over to the principal and in a very rational way inform him of his promise.
5. Cuss him out to his face.
6. Go over to the principal and tell him that he had better give you the position or else.
7. Just forget the matter. After all, the other teacher should be much more qualified anyway.
8. ______________________________

____

Case Study Number 5-9

YOUR REACTION WHEN CONFRONTED WITH ANOTHER IN A LONG LIST OF EXTRA-CURRICULAR ASSIGNMENTS

1. Leave anyway without saying you won't be there.
2. Tell the principal you have other plans.

3. Cancel your plans and stay to flip pancakes cheerfully.
4. Try to find someone to substitute for you.
5. Stay to flip pancakes, but gripe all the time you're there.
6. Say "you're sorry, but you understood that you were hired to teach —not to be a short order cook," and go ahead with your previous plans.
7. ____________________

____

____

Case Study Number 5-10

EXPERIENCING TOO MUCH WORK AND TOO MUCH PRESSURE, YOU ARE ASKING FOR A REDUCTION IN YOUR WORKLOAD AND A REVISION OF YOUR WORK SCHEDULE

1. Try to convince the administration that this workload is not desirable for the children. The schedule is too demanding and the children are not adequately benefiting from the amount of time they are spending in a class. Less time on the subject could be used more beneficially. Interest would not lag, and, therefore, desire and motivation would be stimulated.
2. Suggest that you are not realizing your potential as a teacher due to this excessive pressure. Too many hours and a tight schedule wear on your health, your patience, your general outlook toward your classes and the students. You feel that to be more effective as a teacher your workload should be lightened.
3. Back down. Assure administration that you love your job and the students and that your suggestion was just an idea, one you had not really thought out seriously.
4. ____________________

____

Case Study Number 5-11

YOU DISAGREE WITH RECOMMENDED BOOK LIST

1. Accept the list and follow it closely.
2. Make your views known to the principal.
3. Ask if you may supplement the list with books of your own.
4. Keep books which are not on the list in your room as additional reference materials. Seldom use books on the list.
5. ____________________

____

Case Study Number 5-12

CHOOSING TEXTS

1. You examine and comply with board member's wishes.
2. You examine again but tell the administrator your original choice remains.
3. You reiterate your choice, underlining the fact that you've already looked at a number of series.
4. You give both series to the administrator asking him to make the choice.
5. You enlist the support of other teachers.
6. ______________________________

____

____

Case Study Number 5-13

BUDGET CUT IN YOUR AREA

1. Forget the whole matter and function within the slashed budget.
2. Bring the matter to the attention of your students.
3. Make an appeal to the parents of your students—PTA.
4. Prepare a department report and approach the administrators rationally, armed with statistics.
5. Quit the school!
6. Requisition supplies as a department, recognizing that as a body you may be able to cut down waste and cost.
7. Request that your students purchase certain supplies on their own.
8. Investigate new supply sources—natural materials perhaps? Supplies for free from various companies, etc., i.e., use initiative!
9. ______________________________

____

____

Case Study Number 5-14

YOUR REACTION TO A PRINCIPAL WHO DOES NOT CARRY THROUGH WITH AN ACTION HE HAS INDICATED HE WOULD COMPLETE

1. Assume that the principal has simply forgotten your request and go to him again.
2. Go to the teachers in the building and ask them to share the materials with you.

3. Go beyond your principal to higher administrative authority and request these materials.
4. Get along with what you have.
5. ______________________________

____

Case Study Number 5-15

PREJUDICE AGAINST LOW ACHIEVERS

1. The teacher may try to enlist the support of outside influences, such as parents, superintendents of other districts, as well as of the same district, or publicity in the form of a letter to the editor of the local paper, in order to bring pressure upon the principal. However, any such effort would not necessarily bring about the desired change from "worse" to "better." On the contrary, the actions could backfire. If a teacher is willing to expose another, he has to be willing to accept the consequences of such an act. If he loses, he loses more than his job. He may lose the children, also, if he is busy campaigning all the time against the principal and trying to devise schemes to accomplish his end and thus is too preoccupied to really help the children, his students and responsibility.
2. A slower, but surer, way to improve this situation would be to take inventory of what he had, i.e., the children, and teach them all that they were capable of learning and make do with the materials available. After having "proved" himself to the principal, he might be in a position to wield a few things in the children's favor. Also, he might be able to arrange a borrowing system with the other teachers for the books needed by teaching the subjects to his students at a differently scheduled time. Also, he might be able to find a sponsor willing to provide the children with additional supplies of paper, pencils, crayons, etc. In this manner, he would be concretely improving the situation without cutting his own throat, and his students also would have a better chance.
3. ______________________________

____

Case Study Number 5-16

ADMINISTRATOR OBSERVES YOUR CLASS

1. Change your teaching techniques to fit the administrator's expectations.
2. Do not say anything; it is safer that way.
3. Discuss the differences with your supervisor; ask what he might suggest.

4. Tell the supervisor to stay out of your class; it disrupts the regular routine.
5. Ask him if there is another way to be observed, and explain why.
6. Tell him this is always the way your class is run and continue to teach your way when he is not there.
7. ______________________________

____

Case Study Number 5-17

YOUR REACTION TO THE ADMINISTRATOR'S CRITICISM OF YOUR TEACHING METHODS IN THE CLASSROOM

1. Remain as calm as possible and ask that he wait until the class is over to discuss the matter in private.
2. Overlook the incident in class and go on teaching as though he had said nothing.
3. Tell him he has no right to confront you in class and ask him politely to leave.
4. ______________________________

____

Case Study Number 5-18

YOUR DECISION ON HOW BEST TO TEACH STUDENTS WHO WILL NOT LEARN IN THE TRADITIONAL WAY

1. Resign in favor of a more creative environment.
2. Discuss the matter with several teachers in the department.
3. Write several thoroughly-planned additions to the English curriculum and present them to the principal.
4. Due to the high motivation of the students, you allow the activities to continue unchanged.
5. Ask the students to appear more disciplined and orderly when the principal visits the class.
6. ______________________________

____

Case Study Number 5-19

HANDLING OF CONTROVERSIAL ISSUES IN CLASS

1. Point out to the principal that the handling of such issues is part of the educational process.

2. Tell the principal that there has been no objection from parents.
3. Stop the discussions without defending your previous action.
4. Secure the support of other teachers for your discussions and make their stand known to the principal.
5. Suggest to the principal that he visit the class to see how an issue is handled.
6. Continue the discussions but ask the principal for his approval of the topic.
7. ______________________________

____

Case Study Number 5-20

PARENT SAYS YOU'RE TEACHING CREEPING SOCIALISM

1. Ignore the "speech" and change the subject.
2. Attack his view forcefully.
3. Ask for other students to involve themselves in the question of "those who can, do—etc.," getting a discussion going.
4. Send the student to the vice-principal for discipline because of insubordination.
5. Agree with the student.
6. Tell him *he's* the one who's "inexperienced," and not you.
7. Ask him why he thinks what he said is true.
8. Ask that the student be moved to a different teacher's class.
9. ______________________________

____

Case Study Number 5-21

PRINCIPAL ASKS YOU TO STOP GIVING OPINIONS IN CLASS

1. Try to become more objective.
2. Continue, but be more subtle.
3. Talk to parent(s) who called.
4. State your views to the principal.
5. ______________________________

____

Case Study Number 5-22

DISCUSSION OF SEX IN CLASS

1. Promise the principal that you will stop discussing such controversial issues in your classes.

2. Tell the principal that his request is an infringement on academic freedom and you will continue to teach as you feel you should teach.
3. Do not give your principal a firm answer and register your complaint with your teachers' organization.
4. See your attorney to find out exactly what your rights are in this case.
5. Meet with those parents who support your position on this matter and present your views to the school board.
6. Leave the school system in search of another job.
7. ______________________________

____

____

Case Study Number 5-23

STUDENT ACTIVISM VERSUS PRINCIPAL

1. Discuss individual rights and group responsibility with your classes.
2. Have the "demonstrations" in class.
3. Drop the idea.
4. Give your views to the principal.
5. ______________________________

____

____

Case Study Number 5-24

ROLE CONFLICT: POLICEMAN OR TEACHER?

1. Ignore most of the regulations that you can. Let the students take their own responsibility with what they do.
2. Discuss the situation with your students. Have them give their opinions on the rules and on the teachers as rule enforcers. Help them develop a system by which they can enforce the rules themselves.
3. Organize the teachers to protest to the principal and to the school board, if necessary, their punitive roles. Organize a committee to simplify the regulations and the enforcement procedure.
4. Stop the students from doing what is wrong but do not further refer them to the principal. This way you become a counselor or mediator but not the near-end of a hickory stick.
5. ______________________________

____

____

Case Study Number 5-25

YOUR REACTION UPON BEING CRITICIZED BY AN ADMINISTRATOR FOR ACTING AGAINST SCHOOL POLICY

1. Attempt to understand the administrator's position and hope that you will never catch anybody again.
2. Reveal your own criticism of administrative policy with regard to discipline and perhaps incur a continued conflict with the administration.
3. Discuss the incident with the administrator and try to reach some sort of agreement which is acceptable to both sides, or try to show that perhaps there are exceptions to the rule which you (and other teachers) feel justify action that does not strictly adhere to the normal procedure.
4. Subject your own ideas to strict adherence to expected action; cool it and hope for a change in administration.
5. ______________________________

____

Case Study Number 5-26

SMOKING AND POSSESSION OF TOBACCO ON SCHOOL GROUNDS

1. Try to forget the incident as there is little you can do about it anyway.
2. Talk to Mrs. Jones and let her know your feelings on the matter.
3. Talk to the principal and let him know your position on this matter.
4. Discuss the matter in class with your students and follow the course of action agreed upon in class.
5. Discuss the matter in class with your students but do not follow this discussion with any action as you are a teacher and should be detached.
6. Talk to the other girls, that is those with Ann, inform them of your position and offer to work with their parents to correct the situation.
7. Take this matter to your next teachers' meeting.
8. Take this matter to your teachers' organization.
9. ______________________________

____

Case Study Number 5-27

ENFORCEMENT OF DRESS CODE

1. Ignore the students and carry on as if nothing is amiss.
2. Send the nine young men to the vice-principal's office for an infraction of dress regulations.

3. You have no real sympathy with the new dress regulations but you realize that you cannot ignore the flaunting of the rules in this flagrant manner so you send the students to the vice-principal's office.
   (a) you do not let the students know that you are in sympathy with them.
   (b) you let the students know that you feel the regulations are too rigid and you suggest ways to go about having them changed.
4. Ascertain class opinions and attempt to "lead" the discussion in such a way that the nine young men are seen as transgressors and then send them to the office.
5. Leave the class in charge of the class president and immediately consult the school principal. Follow his instructions whether you agree or not.
6. Attempt, through questioning, to find out who were the instigators of the notion of the patch pockets. The names of the instigators should then be turned in to the principal.
7. Attempt to understand how the students feel since they find it necessary to "interpret" the new dress regulations. You realize that this procedure involves risks but you are willing to take them. Eventually, you feel you will have to enforce the school rulings even though you or the students feel they are arbitrary.
8. Find out what other teachers are going to do and act accordingly.
9. Ask for a teacher conference to consider changing the dress regulations.

10. ____

____

Case Study Number 5-28

YOUR HANDLING OF THE PRINCIPAL'S REQUEST THAT YOU TELL YOUR CLASSES THAT YOU DIDN'T REALLY MEAN WHAT YOU SAID ABOUT MARIJUANA

1. You agree to retract the statements.
2. You defend your viewpoint and refuse to discuss the matter with the class but agree to speak with the boy.
3. You agree to retract with no intention of doing so in the hope that the matter will be dropped.
4. You attempt to work a compromise in which you strongly warn your students of the possible dangers of marijuana without having to change your statements about the present laws.

5. ____

____

Case Study Number 5-29

PRINCIPAL QUESTIONS YOU ON DISCIPLINE PROBLEMS

1. Try to smooth things over so that there is no more conflict than necessary between you and the administrator.
2. State that if the students had been disciplined by the administrator at the beginning of the year there would have been little trouble with others.
3. Ask the administrator for advice on how to deal with future discipline problems.
4. ______________________________

____

Case Study Number 5-30

DISAGREEMENT OVER DISCIPLINE

1. Try to create some sort of force of discipline among the students themselves so that social control comes from peers.
2. Try to talk to the vice-principal about the need for treatment of behavior problems.
3. You yourself punish: give extra homework, threaten failure grades, keep after school, etc.
4. Apply for a transfer.
5. Try to get support among teachers; get a teacher force behind you to apply pressure on the vice-principal.
6. Talk to the principal telling him of the breakdown of control and communication.
7. Take the problem to the PTA hoping the parents will back you in the need for order and thus pressure the administration to treat the behavior problems.
8. ______________________________

____

Case Study Number 5-31

YOUR RESPONSE TO AN ADMINISTRATOR'S COMPLAINT OR CHARGE OF YOUR LACK OF CLASS CONTROL

1. Although you refuse to change, since you realize how valuable your class is to your students, you agree to keep down the noise and to close the door.
2. You try to convince the principal of the value of total class involvement in hopes of its future use throughout the school, and vow inwardly to continue your cause.

3. You threaten tactfully to leave the school if not allowed to continue your classes in this way because you feel so strongly on the matter.
4. You suggest that all the teachers meet to discuss the problem of discipline and class stimulation.
5. ____

____

Case Study Number 5-32

PRINCIPAL VISITS CLASS FREQUENTLY THUS DISRUPTING YOUR CLASS

1. You join the principal in creating a relaxed atmosphere by answering the principal on a first name basis.
2. You speak to the principal after class one day and tell him you do not agree with his philosophy of using your first name or making jokes in front of your class.
3. You speak to older teachers in the school and ask them about the principal's practice of visiting your class so often.
4. You dismiss the situation hoping that the principal will discontinue this practice.
5. ____

____

Case Study Number 5-33

ADMINISTRATOR'S HOAX—A BOMB SCARE

1. Ignore the incident as others will take care of the matter.
2. Talk to Mr. Anderson and let him know your feelings on the matter.
3. Talk to the principal about the matter.
4. Discuss the matter in your classes.
5. Take the matter to the next teachers' meeting.
6. ____

____

Case Study Number 5-34

CONTROVERSY OVER TEACHERS' MEETING

1. Discuss the meeting with others to get their opinions—then all of you approach the principal.
2. Wait until the next meeting and then voice your opinion "on the spot."

3. Go to the superintendent of schools and complain about the situation at your school.
4. Talk to the principal alone and ask what can be done in the future concerning the meetings.
5. ______________________________

____

____

Case Study Number 5-35

AN ADMINISTRATOR ASKS TEACHERS FOR HELP ON THE SCHOOL BOND ISSUE

1. Keep your opinion to yourself as the teacher should be detached from such matters.
2. Make your views known to your colleagues and try to get your teachers' organization to unite in favor of the school bond issue.
3. Go directly to the principal and let him know how you feel on the subject.
4. Go to the next board meeting and state your views.
5. Speak to your students about the importance of the bond issue. Discuss the matter in your social studies classes.
6. ______________________________

____

Case Study Number 5-36

THE PRINCIPAL GIVES NEW TEACHERS ADVICE ON BUYING LIQUOR IN TOWN

1. Follow his advice whether or not you agree.
2. Let the principal know at the meeting that you disagree with his view and feel it is unsound advice.
3. Take the matter to your teachers' organization for discussion and possible resolution.
4. Don't openly disagree with the principal but continue to go to liquor stores in the town.
5. Discuss the matter with the owner of the liquor store and urge him to put pressure on the administration, for the town's economy is important to the state of the schools and vice versa.
6. Simply forget the matter for it is not important.
7. ______________________________

____

Case Study Number 5-37

BEER SERVED AT TEACHERS' MEETING IN YOUR HOME

1. Make an apology to the principal for your "mistake" and assure him that it will not happen again.
2. Try to explain to him that in your opinion it is your personal decision what you serve at your home and that the parents should have nothing to do or say about the personal lives of the teachers.
3. Thank him for informing you of the calls and say nothing about it. Next time you will be more careful that word doesn't leak out.
4. ____

____

Case Study Number 5-38

COMMUNITY CENSORSHIP

1. Tell the school board that you know the students and what is good for them in their studies.
2. Call up the parents who complained and try to get them on your side by telling them the purpose of the play.
3. Set up a compromise with the school board to get the parents' permission to see the play.
4. Take your students to another play.
5. ____

____

Case Study Number 5-39

PRINCIPAL REACTS TO YOUR DATING A STUDENT

1. Get indignant and say it was a personal matter and no one's concern but the two of you. Continue to date.
2. Quietly acquiesce and then date carefully on the sly—get invited to dinner at her house, after church go out to lunch, etc.
3. Cool it 'til the term is over and after she is out of your class continue dating.
4. Quit the school and district if necessary.
5. Show that her grades were well-deserved in class on her test scores, etc., and thereby falsify the original claims by the students and parents and disqualify the rest of the argument as irrelevant to the jurisdiction of the administration.
6. ____

____

Case Study Number 5-40

PRINCIPAL THREATENS FIRING UNLESS YOU LOSE WEIGHT

1. Try to lose weight.
2. Tell the principal you will fight it, that you won't accept this kind of treatment.
3. Ask for a different assignment.
4. Resign from the teaching assignment.
5. ______________________________

   ____

Case Study Number 5-41

YOUR REACTION TO AN IRATE ADMINISTRATOR UPON YOUR RESIGNATION

1. Tolerate the uncooperative, negative treatment by your principal, knowing that in a few months you will be out of the school and away from the situation altogether.
2. Speak with him again in an attempt to improve the situation.
3. Go directly to the district superintendent and discuss the situation with him.
4. Resign early accepting the loss in salary rather than enduring the unpleasant situation.
5. Refuse the new offer and stay in your present teaching position for next year.
6. ______________________________

   ____

   ____

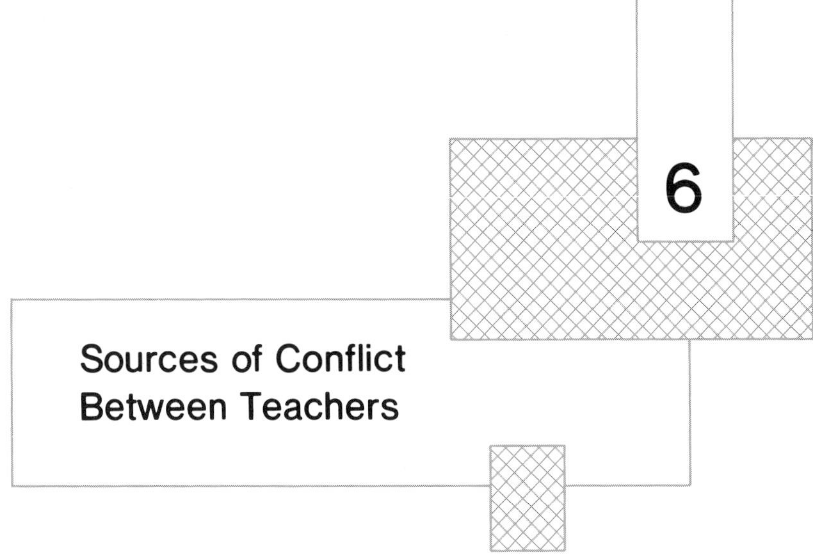

6

Sources of Conflict Between Teachers

Sources of conflict indicate dissatisfaction of teachers with the school as a social system. Such dissatisfaction is also apparent in the relationships established between teachers. One has only to visit the teachers' lounge to recognize intense feelings which many teachers have toward each other. Faculty meetings will on occasion also reveal an inordinate amount of personal conflict. As one faculty member suggested after a faculty meeting, "Just another example of how issues are less important than personality conflicts."

INCONSISTENCY IN DEALING WITH STUDENTS

A constant source of conflict between teachers is the failure on the part of some teachers to discipline students in accordance with written rules and the obsession of other teachers to discipline students. Some teachers abhor the watchdog function and others delight in it. The former are known as "good Joes" who have sold out to the students, and the latter as little dictators. All teachers are extremely aware of the discipline function of schools as is noted in the number of case studies in this section which deal with the matter of discipline. This is understandable, for some teachers are always in danger of losing jobs because of poor discipline.[1]

Harmon Zeigler, a political scientist, notes a connection between teachers who are obsessed with maintaining discipline in our schools and political conservatism. Who are these teachers? According to Zeigler, they are primarily males rather than females. Zeigler argues that most

[1]Willard Waller, *The Sociology of Teaching,* John Wiley & Sons, Inc., New York, 1965, p. 10.

males become more conservative and authoritarian because they don't like their work. This is a result of their being in an establishment basically considered feminine by the public, an establishment where hope for advancement fades with experience.[2]

COMPETITION

Willard Waller writes that ". . . the low state of the profession is partly due to irrelevant competition."[3] It is obvious that competition, both relevant and irrelevant, is expected, if not promoted, between members of a teaching staff. There is always the competition for the hearts and minds of students—especially noticeable in a social system where members constantly interact on a very close basis. One does not simply teach a class or two a day, as is the case with university professors, but instead the teacher lives with his students all day long.

There is a great deal of competition among teachers for the "best" classes. More experienced teachers are usually assigned fast classes and the new teachers are given what are considered to be the dregs. This, incidentally, is one reason for the high turnover among new teachers. Competition also exists for the best materials, for example, books. A new teacher complained to the author that all the good books had been checked out by older teachers at the first day's orientation session. The new teachers didn't even know where the books were kept. Competition for certain rooms, use of the mimeo machine, and use of library books is also common.

Competition also frequently exists between young teachers and those who are older. Older teachers often resent the pushiness of new teachers, and new teachers in turn accuse older teachers of a reluctance to innovate. Young teachers often feel they are better prepared for teaching because they are acquainted, through recent coursework, with the newest trends in thought. Older teachers cite teaching experience as their strong point—something which young teachers do not as yet have. As most school systems honor seniority, young teachers resent the fact that more experienced teachers have special privileges—such as being asked to serve on the most important committees and getting more pay for experience rather than merit teaching.

The dress of teachers is also a source of conflict in many schools. This is not only the result of different age groups but also different socioeconomic levels of teachers. Teachers also argue over student dress codes.

---

[2]Harmon Zeigler, *The Political Life of American Teachers*, Prentice-Hall, Inc., Englewood Cliffs, N. J., 1967, pp. 11-30.
[3]Waller, *op. cit.* [1], p. 353.

Competition also exists between members of different areas of the curriculum. In some schools, mainly suburban schools where the majority of students go on to college, liberal arts teachers look disparagingly on those teaching vocational courses. Some suburban schools were formerly rural schools. While a rural school, the agriculture teacher had a great deal of prestige, but when the school became suburban the same teacher had little prestige, his agriculture classes becoming gardening classes for future suburban home owners. In some schools athletic coaches have a good deal of prestige; in others their prestige is lower than that of first-rate teachers who prepare students for college.

All teachers compete for the time of the students. Those teachers who assign a large amount of homework and work with the students a great deal in extra curricular areas are frequently resented by other teachers. The drama teacher may work with students three hours an afternoon or evening in order to prepare for the next play, the coach may take his athletes away from school for athletic events, and the yearbook sponsor may also demand a great deal of time from his students. Any request for time of the students which is out of the ordinary is suspect and exposes the teacher involved to criticism.

Different teachers appeal to different types of students. One teacher's favorite student will be another teacher's problem student. Teachers, naturally thinking that other teachers react to students as they do, fight for some students and against others, much of this conflict occurring in the teachers' lounge or lunch room. Once again the closeness of members of the school as a social system lends itself to such conflict. There is a good deal of "backbiting" in many school systems. Teachers talk about each other in front of fellow teachers, administrators, and at times, students. If administrators employ favoritism, teachers become jealous of the favorite.

The teachers' lounge and lunch room also provide the milieu in which conflict occurs because of religious and political differences. Social conflict also frequently results over the issues of the use of tobacco and alcohol. Whether or not the teacher joins the "right" teachers' organization is another source of conflict. One issue which is always in the background is that of male teachers versus female teachers. Some males object because females receive equal pay; others object because female teachers are relatively inactive politically in the school system.

There seems to be a feeling among teachers that each teacher should carry his fair load of work. Extra curricular duties are shirked by some teachers, thus causing conflict with other teachers. This occurs even though teachers often object to supervising extra curricular activities.

Finally, there is on some faculties conflict between teachers because of racial and ethnic backgrounds. These conflicts are usually not blatant but are instead subtle as indicated in some of the following case studies.

Case Study Number 6-1

INNOVATOR SEEKS WAYS TO INITIATE CHANGE

You are new, idealistic, and full of ideas. How do you best go about initiating some new ideas among the older teachers without raising antagonism?

Case Study Number 6-2

DEPARTMENT CHAIRMAN ASKS FOR LESSON PLANS FOR EACH NEW IDEA

It is your first teaching assignment and you are determined to use many innovations. The chairman of your department has been teaching for thirty years and is skeptical about any new techniques. Being a chairman, she asks all first-year teachers to submit for approval any lesson plan which deviates from normal procedure.

How do you handle this situation?

Case Study Number 6-3

SHORTAGE OF VOCATIONAL COURSES

You are a teacher of business subjects in a small high school. The courses in the curriculum tend to be academic and the classes are small. Few of the students who graduate go on to college. The chairman of the department is one of the oldest members of the faculty in terms of years in service. Because of his own training and philosophy of education, he has resisted the expansion of the curriculum into strictly vocational types of courses, such as secretarial, clerical, etc. You feel that we need more of these courses since they always seem to be filled, and you try to convince him of this. He maintains that the business curricula should be designed basically to serve the college preparatory students who will be entering such fields as business administration and economics. The other courses are of secondary importance. Since the number of possible course offerings is small, due to limited faculty and budget, the only way to increase the vocational offering is to reduce the academic selection. This, he opposes. The department is evenly divided on the issue; the older members tending to side with the chairman. You feel that many of the students are not able to secure useful business skills because of the shortage of courses in the vocational area and you would like to do something about it.

What will you do?

Case Study Number 6-4

DISAGREEMENT OVER BLACK HISTORY

You are teaching in a primarily Black high school where several racial conflicts have arisen. Several of the students come to you and complain that when they asked the history teacher why they couldn't spend more time with Afro-American history he said that they had a special week for that and that he couldn't find more time in the present curriculum schedule.

What do you do?

Case Study Number 6-5

YOUR REACTION TO THE PORTRAYAL OF THE BLACK IN ANOTHER TEACHER'S CLASS

You are a member of the teaching staff. You attend an assembly given by students in the senior English class. The students present a skit on Macbeth. Students have blackened their faces and use "Negro dialect" throughout the skit. The school is an all-white suburban high school.

What will your reaction be?

Case Study Number 6-6

YOUR REACTION WHEN ANOTHER TEACHER CHANGES HIS CURRICULUM

It disturbs you when you learn from a third party that a fellow teacher is omitting from his course what you consider a very crucial chapter in the course, the content of which is very important to the student's background. It is so close to the end of the school year that the matter needs attention immediately, if at all.

What would you do?

Case Study Number 6-7

YOUR RESPONSE TO ANOTHER TEACHER'S INTERPRETATION OF A BOOK

You are a secondary school teacher. Another teacher gives an absolute interpretation of a book in his class. His students come to your class, tell you of the other teacher's interpretation, and ask for yours. You find the other teacher's interpretation ridiculous.

What do you say?

Case Study Number 6-8

INTERFERENCE WITH GUEST TEACHER

You invite another teacher to show his slides of Europe. When slides of East and West Berlin are shown, he becomes rather emotional about how terrible the Communists are. The students become interested in the Wall, the guards, etc., so the discussion centers upon this one subject. You fear that if you comment, the personal debate between teachers would destroy order and respect for yourself in the classroom.

How will you respond?

Case Study Number 6-9

YOUR REACTION TO TEACHER'S BIAS AGAINST YOUR SHOWING A FILM

You are one of two teachers in your department in a high school. Both of you follow a very similar plan of study in which you combine classes to show periodic films after which you hold a mass discussion. You face conflict when you wish to show a politically biased film, already approved by the administration but adamantly opposed by your fellow social studies teacher. The film offends his personal political views so that he finds it intolerable and insists upon not showing it to either class. You feel that the film would be very valuable material for student discussion.

How would you handle the situation?

Case Study Number 6-10

DISAGREEMENT OVER TEACHER'S UNORTHODOX APPROACH

A young male history teacher desires that his students achieve an understanding of the modern world through comprehension of relatively contemporary forces which are forming it. In supplement to the departmental World History text, he brings to class thirty-five copies each of Hegel's *Reason in History,* Marx' and Engels' *The Manifesto of the Communist Party,* and also Orwell's *1984.* The teacher feels that Hegel's work is valuable because it makes history definitive as it states the methods of writing history, the basis of history (reason), and the purpose and course of world history. The *Manifesto* is important, he contends, because too few people have ever bothered to read the work and compare what was proposed in it to what has, in fact, been adopted. Also, how many people can distinguish between socialism and communism, between helping out the "low-dog" and becoming a member of the "high-dogs"? *1984* is illuminating because it parodies by exaggeration forces at work in the world today.

However, another member of the history department, Mr. Hall, is appalled at his colleague's unorthodoxy. A member of a very conservative local group, Mr. Hall zealously believes that communists are to be decried against, not read. Anyone propagating Marx in the classroom, under any circumstances, he concludes, must be a communist too. After all, the communists are lurking everywhere—in government, in factories, why not the schools? Surely, they can do more damage there with young, impressionable minds to work on and corrupt. Mr. Hall's distrust and fear of his colleague grows until word gets out that one of the teachers in the history department is a "commie." Mr. Hall organizes a group of anxious teachers and parents who confront the "red" history teacher and demand that he quit "indoctrinating" the students by allowing them to read Marx, unadulterated, or resign. In effect, they want their children to be taught that communism is an evil. Let the children be told about communism, but don't let them read its philosophy first-hand.

How can a teacher interested in ideas first, and evaluations second, intellectually communicate with a fellow teacher ruled solely by his emotions, his fears?

Case Study Number 6-11

A FELLOW TEACHER CRITICIZES YOUR TEACHING METHODS

For the past week you and your fellow teachers have had a chance to visit each other's classes. A teacher from another department confronts you after visiting one of your classes. He disagrees with your method of conducting the class and your way of handling the students. In general, he seems to disagree with your whole philosophy of teaching.

After listening to these criticisms, what is your reaction? How do you respond to this person?

Case Study Number 6-12

COLLEAGUE CRITICIZES YOUR TEACHING

You are a faculty member on a secondary school staff. It comes to your attention that the teacher next door to you is making negative comments to students, the principal, other teachers, and parents concerning your teaching capability.

What do you do?

Case Study Number 6-13

STUDENTS TALK ABOUT TEACHERS IN COLLEAGUE'S CLASS

You are a teacher and you find out from students that a colleague has allowed gossip about other teachers to dominate the class period.

What would you do?

Case Study Number 6-14

CONDUCT IN THE HALL

There is supposed to be a rule about running in the hallways and talking in the hallway during school hours. Your class discusses this and comes up with sound reasons why they should adhere to these rules.

However, it becomes evident that certain teachers disregard these rules and with no respect for other teachers and classes allow raucous behavior in the halls.

How do you explain this to your own class? How do you "get the point across" with the teachers in question?

Case Study Number 6-15

CONFLICT WITH TEACHER WHO KEEPS STUDENTS AFTER THE BELL

You're new. The teacher who has most of your 6th period class invariably releases them from 5th period long after the bell. The kids can't make it comfortably to your class on time and consequently you have them drifting in up to 5 minutes late (40-minute classes); the other teacher is generally respected.

What will you do?

Case Study Number 6-16

YOUR REACTION TO TEACHERS' OBJECTIONS TO YOUR PROPOSED FIELD TRIP

You are a member of the English department. You are planning to take your students to see a play in a local theater—a play the class is currently studying. The class is looking forward to the performance and you have secured the permission of the administration and the parents. However, some fellow teachers object to this field trip because students will be absent from their classes that day. They suggest that you cancel the field trip in order to prevent discord among the faculty.

What would be your reaction to their suggestion?

Case Study Number 6-17

COLLEAGUE ASSIGNS A GREAT DEAL OF HOMEWORK

You are a teacher whose third period class is chiefly made up of students from Miss X's ninth grade second period class. Miss X prides herself on having a philosophy best expressed in the maxim: "An idle mind is the devil's workshop." She gives a great deal of homework which you consider "busywork." Your students almost always enter complaining about Miss X. One day you are asked if you can't "do something."

What would your reaction be?

Case Study Number 6-18

PRESSURE FROM FOOTBALL COACH

You are planning to give a "D" to Jim Starr in your 12th grade class. The football coach approaches you and explains that a "D" on Jim's mid-semester report will make him ineligible for the three remaining football games. As Jim is the star quarterback, this will almost surely cost the school the league championship. Further, the coach points out to you that Jim will do better after the league season is over and will have time to pull up his grade in your class. You doubt this as Jim's "D" is none too solid as it is but you also realize that playing football has been a primary factor in keeping Jim in school up to now.

What do you tell the coach?

Case Study Number 6-19

YOUR REACTION TO ANOTHER TEACHER'S APPARENTLY INEFFECTIVE HANDLING OF A STUDENT

You are a first year teacher in a fairly loosely structured school. Your class is composed of many students who have consistently been labeled discipline problems by their previous teachers. You are able to establish good rapport with your students, however, and are encountering few problems. In fact, Lonnie, who is a very slow pupil and who has previously been labeled a severe discipline problem, is making a great deal of progress in your class.

During the year, a departmentalized reading program is launched, and Lonnie is sent to another room one hour a day for reading instruction. His new reading teacher is a veteran in the school with a reputation for being quite permissive. Soon you are receiving daily reports from this teacher that Lonnie is making no progress and is, in fact, a deterrent to the progress of other students in the room. He is reportedly doing such things as hiding in the wastebasket and refusing to get out, hiding other children's materials and refusing to tell where they are, moving about the room at will, etc. The teacher asks for your help in remedying this situation.

Upon confronting Lonnie with this report of his behavior, his only comment is "but she lets me."

What should you do?

Case Study Number 6-20

COLLEAGUE GIVES ADVICE ABOUT ONE OF YOUR STUDENTS

You are a new teacher in school, and you are waiting in the teachers' lounge for the first day of classes to begin. You overhear a conversation among the teachers there. They are talking about one of the students in the class you will be teaching. A teacher who is respected in the school says that this is the worst student. You are already prejudiced toward this pupil before meeting him.

What is your reply?

Case Study Number 6-21

THE USE OF ART CLASS EQUIPMENT

As a second year art teacher you have observed that a senior member of your department is not using certain facilities for printmaking which appear to be stored in her room. You feel, with your particular background, that you could make use of this equipment. However, you and this other teacher don't quite see eye-to-eye about teaching techniques and she resents the free atmosphere in your classroom and the sorts of results that you have been achieving with your students. All in all, she seems to feel threatened by your enthusiasm, approach, etc. Things are somewhat strained between you.

How would you deal with this teacher to establish a better rapport and how would you handle the matter of the equipment?

Case Study Number 6-22

TEACHER LEAVES YOUR CLASSROOM IN A MESS

One teacher in the school must move from classroom to classroom because of a lack of classrooms available. This teacher uses your classroom one period a day. After each use your room is a mess. Desks are written on, gum is stuck on the bottom of the desks, and paper is scattered on the floor.

What should you do?

Case Study Number 6-23

YOUR REACTION TO A PERSONAL ATTACK BY ANOTHER TEACHER WHO RESENTS YOUR POSITION

You are young and a fairly new teacher at a school. You have received the position of department chairman because of your educational background and training even though you are younger and have less experience than several others who had desired the position. Because you are expected to evaluate other teachers in the department, you are resented by one teacher who tries to embarrass you and make you uncomfortable in your job. The situation places a great deal of pressure on you because you know that several others are in sympathy with the resentful teacher.

How will you handle this conflict?

Case Study Number 6-24

YOUR REACTION TO A DEPARTMENT CHAIRMAN WHO IS NOT CONSCIENTIOUS

You are a new teacher in the school. The only person with whom you have become acquainted is the principal himself. You come to school on orientation day and the principal introduces you to your department chairman. The chairman waits until the principal leaves and then informs you that you have officially met with him for the last time. There will be no department meetings this year. He further states that you are to supply yourself with whatever materials you might need from the school or by ordering them through regular channels. He closes with the following: "And oh yes, good luck!"

What will your reaction be?

Case Study Number 6-25

A FEW TEACHERS GET "BEST" CLASSES

You are just completing your first year at a new school after a few years of teaching experience, and the division of classes is being decided for the next year. It seems that for next year, as it was for this year, the department chairman and a couple of other teachers have most of the good classes, with the remaining teachers taking the rest.

What do you do?

Case Study Number 6-26

YOUR REACTION TO A MEMBER OF YOUR DEPARTMENT WHO "DOESN'T GIVE A DAMN"

One of the members of your department is obviously not bothering with his job. He considers his students to be completely unworthy of his capabilities and is, therefore, merely putting in time to collect his pay.

What will your reaction be?

Case Study Number 6-27

YOUR REACTION TO JEALOUSY ON THE PART OF A FELLOW TEACHER

You are a young female teacher who has been given three periods of team teaching, with an older, more experienced teacher as the head of the team. She is respected by the students, but she is a very strict disciplinarian, and very distant with them; therefore, they have little personal contact with her. Because you are young, pretty, sympathetic, and easy to talk to, most of the students seem to come to you with their comments and problems. After some time of this you notice a marked change in the older teacher's attitude toward you. Whereas before she had been friendly and helpful, she now seems to be snubbing you, and even trying to undermine your position on the team, by continuously pointing out any errors you happen to make. After some thought you realize that she resents the fact that the students seem to like you better.

What do you do?

Case Study Number 6-28

PERSONALITY CONFLICT IN TEAM-TEACHING SITUATION

As a teacher you are put in a team-teaching position with teachers from two other departments. You manage to get along with the one teacher and the two of you work well together. The other teacher is a different story. There is a conflict in personalities and in ideas of how the team should work. It has gotten to the point where personal antagonisms will soon hinder both of you in your teaching effectiveness and ability to work as a team. There have been misunderstandings on both your parts and up until now, you have either smoothed them over—or tried to in nice ways. The teacher with whom you get along in some instances acted as mediator between the two of you, but she too is anxious about the antagonisms.

What would you do?

Case Study Number 6-29

TEAM-TEACHING MEMBER IS UNSUCCESSFUL

You are a member of a team-teaching group. You have carefully observed the other teacher and feel that he is being unsuccessful in getting anything across to the students. They aren't motivated by him and this makes your job twice as difficult. Also they aren't learning the material as they should from him and consequently your material is not understood as well.

What could you do to alleviate this situation?

Case Study Number 6-30

TEACHER REVEALS PREJUDICE IN FRONT OF TEACHERS WHO ARE MINORITY GROUP MEMBERS

A teacher from another state had been hired to teach at a junior high school where one half the enrollment is Spanish and Mexican-American. The teachers were planning for their faculty Christmas "get-together." One teacher suggested a beach party swim-in. Another said, "that would be fun; I have never had the opportunity to go swimming at Christmas time." The new teacher remarked "I would like to go to the beach but my skin would tan too dark and then I may be mistaken for one of these Mexicans around here." Everyone looked surprised but no one commented. There were three Spanish teachers present. The teacher quickly said, "Oh, I didn't mean your kind, you are different from them." Still no response from the others. The teacher left the room in a hurry. Everyone just looked at each other but no one spoke.

What would you do?

Case Study Number 6-31

FELLOW TEACHER PREJUDICED AGAINST MINORITY GROUP STUDENTS

The high school where you are a social studies teacher has a small minority of Blacks and Mexican-Americans in attendance. These minority students seem to socialize mainly within their own groups, but are widely accepted in sports activities. From low-class homes, these students generally do not do the quality work of the white upper-class children who also attend the school. However, the school has not yet been divided into classes of low, high, and average, so that every teacher has some of these students in his classes each year. Although the presence of these students makes it difficult for the conscientious teacher to preach the standard middle-class values and experiences, some teachers at the school ignore the whole problem entirely by preaching conformity to middle-class ideals and aspirations and clamping down on the different feelings of the minority students. One teacher in particular reinforces his own security and status quo by making certain that the minority students conform to his expectations. Not only is he a teacher who will not take the minority students into consideration as real human beings with problems very different from his own, but he is, on top of that, a freshman English instructor, and in this position he further stifles these students' freedom of expression.

Unhappy with what this situation is doing to the minority students and to the attitudes of the student body as a whole, what would you do?

Case Study Number 6-32

YOUR REACTION TO TEACHER OF SEX EDUCATION

A teacher at Ansen High School became very upset over the sex education class when he saw a word list his daughters had to memorize. The list included such words as "erection, nocturnal emission, ejaculation, masturbation, contraceptives, etc." The disturbing part was that the class was coeducational. The teacher talked to the daughters and learned that the class discussed quite frankly the items on the word list. They also indicated that there was some embarrassment on the part of some girls to participate in class discussion.

The teacher decided to talk to the principal and the teacher of the sex education class to learn more about it. The principal was equally shocked over the word list and was quite surprised that these things would be discussed coeducationally.

Several noon meetings were set up to learn more about the course. Dr. Barnard, leading obstetrician in the area, was consulted on the course content and he expressed considerable concern over the class being taught coeducationally. He supported the need for sex education but felt it could be handled more effectively with the boys meeting separately from the girls. The teacher of the class did not share this opinion. He felt it was more wholesome and natural for both boys and girls to be present to discuss the intimacies of sex life. Discussions would become quite personal as they would relate to different contraceptives and their effectiveness. Even the comfort of wearing a preventative by the boy was talked about in the class.

You are a teacher in the school. How would you react to this situation?

Case Study Number 6-33

DIFFERING INTERPRETATIONS ON USE OF DRUGS

Another teacher on the staff has been informing his students that marijuana is a dangerous, physically-addictive drug that causes permanent brain damage and chromosome mutation, and that it leads to more serious drug addiction which will ultimately put one in a mental hospital. Some of your former students are in his class. In your class, these students had thoroughly investigated the dangers of marijuana and had concluded that there is not yet enough evidence about the physical hazards to form any final conclusions. They had also concluded from studies that marijuana does not seem to have a cause-effect relationship with stronger drugs. These students have come to you for an answer.

What will you say?

Case Study Number 6-34

YOUR REACTION TO A TEACHER SMOKING MARIJUANA

At a private party which you attend there are several teachers present. One deliberately lights up a marijuana cigarette.

What is your reaction?

Case Study Number 6-35

POLITICAL DISAGREEMENT IN FACULTY ROOM

You are in the faculty staff room having coffee. You are a new member of the staff. A fellow teacher expounds on his political views (to no one in particular). You disagree with his politics.

What would you do?

Case Study Number 6-36

FELLOW TEACHER IS UNCOUTH

Mr. Cabe, a fellow teacher, does many distasteful things but among the worst are his table manners. It has reached a point to where the other staff members, with the exception of one, refuse to eat at the same table or be in the same room while he's "slopping down his grub."

He's constantly talking, especially when his mouth is full of food. And with the aid of one missing front tooth, he is anything but tidy. He doesn't seem to be able to take the hint as to why the others leave the teachers' dining room and go back to their classrooms to eat.

What do you suggest?

RESPONSES TO CASES

Case Study Number 6-1
INNOVATOR SEEKS WAYS TO INITIATE CHANGE

1. Don't bother, merely be "an example."
2. Don't even let them know indirectly that you're out of the traditional lines.
3. Try to involve others who will then use your ideas.
4. Be sure to have your students let their parents know how good your innovations are.
5. ______________________________

____

____

Case Study Number 6-2
DEPARTMENT CHAIRMAN ASKS FOR LESSON PLANS FOR EACH NEW IDEA

1. You take this problem to the principal.
2. You discuss this problem with other teachers in the school.
3. You agree with the chairman that new teachers do not have enough experiences and should have their lesson plans checked.
4. You listen to the chairman but return to your classroom to plan a new program with no intention of discussing it with the chairman.
5. ______________________________

____

Case Study Number 6-3
SHORTAGE OF VOCATIONAL COURSES

1. As a means of convincing the chairman as to the importance of this curriculum change, prepare a brief questionnaire and distribute it to the business establishments in the community.
2. Confer with the principal (who is in his first year at this school) in an effort to elicit his support on curriculum change.
3. Speak individually with department members. Urge those who are sympathetic to try to persuade those who are not.
4. Have a departmental party and try to prevail with good feeling.
5. ______________________________

____

Case Study Number 6-4

DISAGREEMENT OVER BLACK HISTORY

1. You speak to the teacher and try to explain your views and the feelings of the students.
2. You take the situation to the administration.
3. Feeling that neither the teacher nor the administration would do anything, you get word of the situation to certain black community groups who you know will put pressure on the school.
4. ______________________________

____

Case Study Number 6-5

YOUR REACTION TO THE PORTRAYAL OF THE BLACK IN ANOTHER TEACHER'S CLASS

1. Keep your feelings to yourself and hope the matter will be dropped.
2. Talk to the English teacher so that your feelings are made known.
3. Discuss the matter with the high school principal.
4. Use this episode as a topic for discussion in your classes.
5. Talk to the students who presented the skit to find out why they presented it in the way they did.
6. Stand up during the assembly and make your views known to those in attendance.
7. ______________________________

____

Case Study Number 6-6

YOUR REACTION WHEN ANOTHER TEACHER CHANGES HIS CURRICULUM

1. Discuss the matter with the teacher in question.
2. Discuss the matter with the department chairman.
3. Keep it under your hat for now but remember to bring it up when the next year's courses are being planned.
4. Keep it completely to yourself, since you wouldn't like to have other teachers prying in your classroom.
5. Talk to the other teachers about it.
6. ______________________________

____

Case Study Number 6-7

YOUR RESPONSE TO ANOTHER TEACHER'S INTERPRETATION OF A BOOK

1. You make the other teacher look bad by saying that his interpretation is incorrect.
2. You say that there are many interpretations to any subject, and then you give yours.
3. You give your interpretation without comment.
4. You say that you are not dealing with that particular book in your class and so you refuse to comment.
5. You say that you will have to talk to the other teacher before you can give your opinion.
6. ____

____

____

Case Study Number 6-8

INTERFERENCE WITH GUEST TEACHER

1. Say nothing at the moment, but bring up the subject the next day in class.
2. Never mention the teacher's comments to anyone.
3. Try to give a historical perspective on Berlin while the slides are shown, hoping to thus temper the more gruesome aspects.
4. Don't say anything at the moment, but let the other teacher know your displeasure outside of class.
5. Ask the teacher if he could go on to other slides, even though the students are interested in these.
6. Tell him that Berlin is problematical, but he shouldn't be so hard-headed about Communists.
7. Tell the class the next day why you think this teacher is so biased against Communism.
8. Stop the slides and begin a class discussion, hoping to take the attention away from the one teacher.
9. Ask the students to come the next day with information about Berlin, again hoping to discourage the immediate interest in such "atrocities."
10. Ask the teacher not to be so political in such a thing as enjoying slides of Europe.
11. Try to get the teacher's attention and somehow convey that you would like him to go on.
12. Join the discussion, giving your impressions of the Communist police state.

13. Encourage the enthusiasm of the students, but talk about Communism in general, not just the Wall.
14. Tell the principal, should he be of the same political views as you.
15. ______________________________

____

Case Study Number 6-9

YOUR REACTION TO TEACHER'S BIAS AGAINST YOUR SHOWING A FILM

1. Take the problem to the administration to be handled and decided upon.
2. Persuade the offended teacher to let the film be shown to your class only and hold discussion within your class alone.
3. Although you feel the film to be very important, you wish not to offend and alienate your fellow teacher, and agree not to show the film.
4. Try to convince the other teacher of the film's value and your reasons for showing it to both classes (and cry if you don't persuade him). If he still isn't convinced, you suggest that he not watch it and that you will handle the viewing by both classes and subsequent discussion.
5. ______________________________

____

Case Study Number 6-10

DISAGREEMENT OVER TEACHER'S UNORTHODOX APPROACH

1. The "accused" may present a defense for his approach to history to all those interested and especially to Mr. Hall. Explaining the purpose and goal of his teaching, he may convince a few people that he is only interested in presenting the ideas alive in the world today, and that he is not making the students into revolutionaries. Rather, he presents the material and then proceeds to demonstrate the inconsistencies between communist theory and practice, an understanding of which he feels to be necessary to any valid evaluation of the subject. In this manner, by reasoning with the "mob," a few may realize that they didn't look before leaping. Although Mr. Hall will probably never be convinced of the "red's innocence," the situation should calm down and the rumor die out in time.
2. The history teacher could resign without defending himself, but this would be contrary to his intellectual belief that reason rules the

world. Resignation would serve no constructive purpose and he would not be likely to resign merely to pacify Mr. Hall.

3. He could agree to cease using the *Manifesto* in the classroom and use only books *about* Communism and not *of* it, but this action would seriously affect his autonomy as a teacher, and the autonomy of all teachers in general. Therefore, he should hold his ground while under fire and strive for an understanding between himself and his "accusers."
4. ______________________________

____

Case Study Number 6-11

A FELLOW TEACHER CRITICIZES YOUR TEACHING METHODS

1. You are indignant. You tell him that the way you run your class is none of his concern. You suggest he keep his comments and criticisms to himself.
2. You thank him for his suggestions and tell him you will seriously consider changing or modifying your present teaching methods.
3. You can complain to the administration about the visiting program. You can ask that your class not be involved in the program again.
4. ______________________________

____

Case Study Number 6-12

COLLEAGUE CRITICIZES YOUR TEACHING

1. Say nothing and hope that the situation passes.
2. Talk to the teacher in question and ask him what he thinks he is doing.
3. Discuss the problem with the principal.
4. Start saying bad things about him to your students and their parents to see how he likes it.
5. ______________________________

____

Case Study Number 6-13

STUDENTS TALK ABOUT TEACHERS IN COLLEAGUE'S CLASS

1. Go to the principal and tell him what you know. Perhaps he could talk with the teacher in question.

2. Go talk with the teacher yourself.
3. Ignore the issue.
4. Inadvertently instill in the students the difference between constructive criticism and gossip.
5. ______________________________

____

____

Case Study Number 6-14

CONDUCT IN THE HALL

1. Speak directly to the teachers involved.
2. Passively allow the behavior to exist.
3. Explain to your class that the others simply don't understand or have respect for others.
4. Use this as an example of "how not" to behave.
5. Stress personal responsibility.
6. Discuss it with all the teachers at a teachers' meeting.
7. Take it to the principal to do something about it.
8. ______________________________

____

____

Case Study Number 6-15

CONFLICT WITH TEACHER WHO KEEPS STUDENTS AFTER THE BELL

1. Forget it and plan your classes so they begin later.
2. Talk to the teacher.
3. Put pressure on the kids—penalize them for being late so they'll bring pressure on the teacher.
4. Complain to the higher authorities.
5. ______________________________

____

Case Study Number 6-16

YOUR REACTION TO TEACHERS' OBJECTIONS TO YOUR PROPOSED FIELD TRIP

1. Cancel your plans completely.
2. Take the class to the play as scheduled.

3. Try to schedule the trip for a Saturday or holiday.
4. Point out to those faculty members who object the advantages of attending a performance of the play.

5. ____

____

____

Case Study Number 6-17

COLLEAGUE ASSIGNS A GREAT DEAL OF HOMEWORK

1. Tell the class that they should not complain because there will always be Miss X's in the world; that they should learn to accept the bad along with the good, etc.
2. Don't make any promises to the class, but suggest that perhaps you are in a position to influence Miss X.
3. Go to a friend in Miss X's department and discuss the matter.
4. Confront Miss X with what the students are saying and your own feelings about the homework assignments.
5. Try to find out if the homework assignments from Miss X's class are really as "bad" as the students say.
6. At the next teachers' meeting, suggest that the matter of homework (purposes and goals, etc.,) be discussed.
7. Suggest at the next teachers' meeting that it would be a good idea to get some immediate feedback from students re: homework in the form of an anonymous questionnaire.
8. Do nothing, i.e., tell the class that the problem is between it and Miss X, and, therefore, not up for discussion in your class.
9. Plan a role-playing episode in which students play out what they consider opposing points of view regarding homework. Attempt to get students to reverse roles in an effort to increase understanding of the other side.

10. ____

____

____

Case Study Number 6-18

PRESSURE FROM FOOTBALL COACH

1. You refuse his request.
2. You agree with the coach and comply with his request.
3. You tell the coach that Jim's "D" is so low that it would be better for him to talk to another teacher in whose class Jim is also doing

poorly. You add that if the coach cannot persuade the other teacher to change his grade you may reconsider.

4. You are shocked by the coach's request and relate the incident to the high school principal.
5. ______________________________

____

____

Case Study Number 6-19

YOUR REACTION TO ANOTHER TEACHER'S APPARENTLY INEFFECTIVE HANDLING OF A STUDENT

1. Punish Lonnie for his misbehavior in the other room.
2. Indicate to the other teacher that you think she is being too permissive with Lonnie.
3. Indicate to the other teacher that this is her problem.
4. Consult the principal for advice.
5. Ask to have Lonnie transferred back to your room even though the program of reading being taught in your room does not fit his needs.
6. ______________________________

____

____

Case Study Number 6-20

COLLEAGUE GIVES ADVICE ABOUT ONE OF YOUR STUDENTS

1. Ask more questions about the student.
2. Try to forget what the teacher said.
3. Thank her for the information.
4. ______________________________

____

Case Study Number 6-21

THE USE OF ART CLASS EQUIPMENT

1. Approach her directly and ask her if you might make use of the equipment.
2. Suggest an experiment in printmaking—try to work out some sort of team teaching effort to combine your talents.

3. Discuss new horizons—specifically printmaking—in a department meeting.
4. Forget the equipment and concentrate on something else for your students.
5. ______________________________

____

Case Study Number 6-22

TEACHER LEAVES YOUR CLASSROOM IN A MESS

1. Stay in the class and observe what goes on.
2. Correct the class that is causing the problem.
3. Mention the problem to the teacher.
4. Report the problem to the principal.
5. Be quiet about the situation.
6. ______________________________

____

Case Study Number 6-23

YOUR REACTION TO A PERSONAL ATTACK BY ANOTHER TEACHER WHO RESENTS YOUR POSITION

1. Attempt to get along with that teacher as well as possible.
2. Relate the situation to an administrator.
3. Try to placate the resentful teacher by some means.
4. Do your job as well as possible and try to avoid personal confrontations with your antagonist.
5. Confront the person directly; tell him where you stand and that you hope he will cooperate.
6. Consult the entire department in a meeting; explain your position and ideas and ask their assistance for the good of the school.
7. Resign from the position.
8. ______________________________

____

Case Study Number 6-24

YOUR REACTION TO A DEPARTMENT CHAIRMAN WHO IS NOT CONSCIENTIOUS

1. Immediately contact the principal to seek out his advice.
2. Take what materials you need and leave.

3. Proceed with your work under the assumption that he was only jesting and will really give you guidance when needed.
4. Seek help from others in the department.
5. ______________________________

____

Case Study Number 6-25

A FEW TEACHERS GET "BEST" CLASSES

1. Do nothing.
2. Say that you feel that the good and poor classes should be divided more equally among all the teachers.
3. Discuss the problem with other teachers.
4. Go to the principal.
5. ______________________________

____

Case Study Number 6-26

YOUR REACTION TO A MEMBER OF YOUR DEPARTMENT WHO "DOESN'T GIVE A DAMN"

1. Agree completely because you think you're wasting your time too.
2. Get into an argument with him about the value of teaching.
3. Mind your own business.
4. Discuss the "problem teacher" with other teachers.
5. Discuss his attitude with the department chairman or administrator.
6. Be sympathetic—and try to understand that not everyone loves teenagers as much as you do (or pretend to).
7. ______________________________

____

Case Study Number 6-27

YOUR REACTION TO JEALOUSY ON THE PART OF A FELLOW TEACHER

1. Do nothing in the hope that she will soon realize that you are not doing this intentionally, and consequently change her attitude toward you.
2. Speak to her about it and try to work out some sort of an understanding.

3. Discourage students from coming to you hoping they will go to her instead. Or say, "I'm busy. Why don't you go and see Mrs. ________________ instead?"
4. Speak to the rest of the team about it and see if they can help.
5. Speak to the principal about it and ask him to speak to the older woman.

6. ____

____

____

Case Study Number 6-28

PERSONALITY CONFLICT IN TEAM-TEACHING SITUATION

1. Ignore the conflict and try to carry on.
2. Try to be nice and diplomatic and iron things out like two adults.
3. Go to the principal and explain the situation asking for a change in assignment.
4. Have all of the team members get together and discuss the problems realistically, so that some sort of workable arrangement can be found.
5. Have a showdown between the two of you, hoping that personal antagonisms can be put aside for the sake of the students and your team.

6. ____

____

____

Case Study Number 6-29

TEAM-TEACHING MEMBER IS UNSUCCESSFUL

1. Not say anything and hope things will just get better.
2. Tell the principal about the problem.
3. Talk to the other teacher and tell him how you think he should teach the material.
4. Discuss the matter with other teachers.
5. Review with the students what the other teacher has attempted to teach them.
6. Explain to the teacher how you feel and attempt to work out your problems by coming to a closer agreement.

7. ____

____

Case Study Number 6-30

TEACHER REVEALS PREJUDICE IN FRONT OF TEACHERS WHO ARE MINORITY GROUP MEMBERS

1. Change the subject and do not refer to the teacher's remark at any time.
2. Change the subject but return to it when the teacher who made the remark has left.
3. Challenge the teacher's remark on the spot. Let all of the teachers know where you stand on this subject.
4. Have the party and don't invite the teacher who made the remark.
5. ______________________________

____

Case Study Number 6-31

FELLOW TEACHER PREJUDICED AGAINST MINORITY GROUP STUDENTS

1. Ignore the situation as it exists in his class and work doubly hard on the minority students in your own classes.
2. Try to organize the minority students outside of class, giving them an individual expression all their own.
3. Inform your students—both white and minority—of what is going on and get them to organize some kind of protest.
4. Talk to the principal in private about the situation which exists. See if you as a teacher can work out some kind of seminar with the other teachers so that the situation will come out in the open and perhaps solutions can be arrived at.
5. Try to initiate discussion of such problems in a general way at your departmental meetings with the view of making departmental plans for providing avenues of expression to meet the particular needs of the minority students.
6. ______________________________

____

Case Study Number 6-32

YOUR REACTION TO TEACHER OF SEX EDUCATION

1. Detach yourself from the situation as it does not deal with your area of the curriculum.
2. Support the position that sex education classes should be coeducational.

3. Support the position that sex education classes should be segregated by sex.
4. Talk to the teacher of the sex education class and make your views known on the matter.
5. Discuss the matter in your social studies classes.
6. ______________________________

____

Case Study Number 6-33

DIFFERING INTERPRETATIONS ON USE OF DRUGS

1. Tell your students the other teacher is a fanatic.
2. Tell the students to form their own opinions.
3. Give the other teacher some new materials on drugs.
4. Write an editorial for the school newspaper on marijuana.
5. ______________________________

____

Case Study Number 6-34

YOUR REACTION TO A TEACHER SMOKING MARIJUANA

1. You ignore the incident but leave the party soon afterward.
2. You loudly protest the incident so that nobody condemns the teaching profession.
3. You report the teacher to the proper authorities.
4. You feel that what a teacher does in his spare time is none of your business.
5. You see nothing wrong with smoking marijuana cigarettes.
6. You don't say anything but you hope that one of your fellow teachers reports the incident.
7. You talk to the teacher later and ask him why he did such a thing in public.
8. ______________________________

____

Case Study Number 6-35

POLITICAL DISAGREEMENT IN FACULTY ROOM

1. Enter into debate (disagreement).
2. Say nothing to avoid dissension.

3. Catch him alone and discuss his arguments.
4. Change the subject of conversation.
5. Ask another teacher if he agrees with the speaker.
6. ____

____

Case Study Number 6-36

FELLOW TEACHER IS UNCOUTH

1. Refer him to the administrator in charge for a stern, firm suggestion or two.
2. Sit across from him for one day and try to be as messy as he is.
3. Eat elsewhere.
4. Speak to him about his manners.
5. ____

____

____

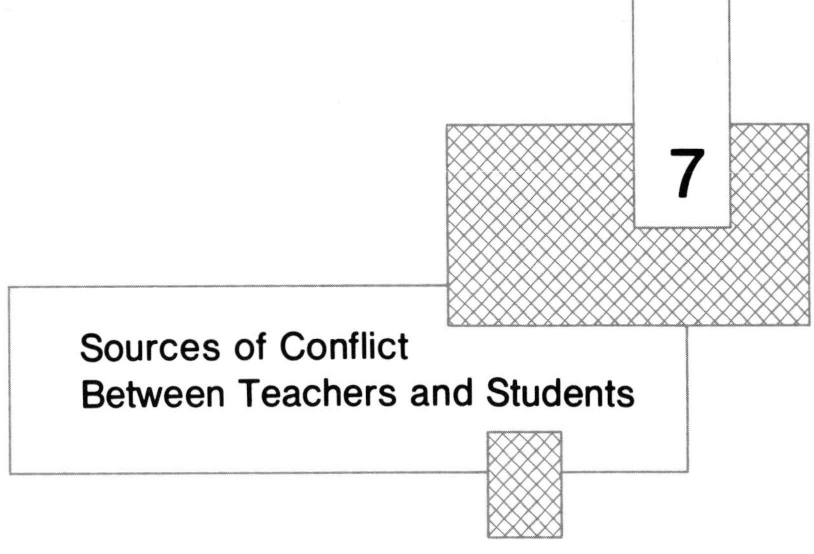

There is no more controversial relationship than that between the teacher and his students. This relationship is not limited to the classroom but instead pervades the entire school. College students, intent on becoming teachers, often fail to see how essentially different the university social system is from that of the public schools. The teacher lives with his students in a manner not readily apparent to the prospective teacher. The teacher encounters students before class in the morning, five hours or more a day in class, and frequently during the noon hour and after school. Little wonder that conflict situations develop between teachers and students.

A REGIMENTED SOCIETY

Students, like many of their teachers, complain for the lack of freedom in their school. Although divergency is an essential quality of creativity, it runs counter to the disposition of many, if not most, schools.[1] The student arrives in the morning, needs tardy and absence slips, library passes, and permission to go to the rest room. In some schools rest rooms are locked between classes and during the lunch period. Students smoke in the rest rooms, thereby requiring the regulation, it is claimed.

The lack of freedom and incentive for creativity is fostered, many students claim, because of their teachers' obsession with busywork and

---

[1]Carl Nordstrom, Edgar Z. Friedenberg, and Hilary A. Gold, *Society's Children: A Study of Ressentiment in the Secondary School,* Random House, New York, 1967, p. 9. For a discussion of areas in which schools try to achieve consensus see Dale L. Brubaker, "Normative Value Judgments and Analysis," *Social Education,* vol. 32, No. 5, 1968, pp. 489-492.

pressure for grades rather than the stimulation of thinking. Students get tired of answering the questions at the end of the chapter.

Some students simply resign themselves to the pressure and wait for freedom after graduation, others resist—the result being a struggle of personalities.[2]

Why is it that teachers frequently become obsessed with the structure of the educational institution at the expense of learning? One reason is that the more divergent views of today's youth pose a threat to the more rigid views of adults and teachers. When threatened, the teacher cannot personally cope with the divergency and therefore becomes more rigid. Evidence that students' beliefs are less rigid and narrow than the views of students in the 1950's is supported by the research of M. Kent Jennings, a political scientist. Jennings reports that today's students are more tolerant of political and social diversity, less chauvinistic, and more cosmopolitan in political orientation.[3] It is little wonder that journalism gives much play to the idea of a generation gap, which in our terms means a gap between the students and their teachers. It is ironic to think that teachers may be culturally disadvantaged compared to students with respect to tolerance for diversity.

GULF BETWEEN SCHOOL RHETORIC AND PRACTICE

On the one hand students are told that they are democracy's hope for the future; on the other hand they are told that they are going to hell for a lack of appropriate values, the intimation being that adults have such values because of their struggle through the depression and two world wars. As one parent said, "If these young people had to face the problems we faced during the depression, they'd throw up their hands and quit."

Students are often told that the school is a training ground for democracy while at the same time the principal says he runs a democratic school. Student councils are often a farce for when the students really get power the administrators and teachers feel threatened—especially if their favorite students are not in power positions. Student courts have been reported to have been abolished when those in power acquitted their friends by accepting pleas of insanity.[4] Yet the school

---

[2]Willard Waller, *The Sociology of Teaching*, John Wiley & Sons, Inc., New York, 1965, p. 339.

[3]M. Kent Jennings, "Pre-Adult Orientations to Multiple Systems of Government," prepared for the Midwest Conference of Political Scientists, April, 1966 (Mimeographed), as cited in John J. Patrick, *Political Socialization of American Youth*, Research Bulletin No. 3 of the National Council for the Social Studies, Washington, D. C., p. 13.

[4]Nordstrom, *op. cit.* [1] p. 41.

persists in its public relations to call the school a democracy in which students are being trained to be "good citizens."[5] Would any principal admit to being a despot, benevolent or not? All of this supports the traditional definition of a teacher as a man hired to tell lies to little boys.[6] Many teachers, administrators, and parents feel that students cannot be given the facts but instead must be instilled with idealism which will be tempered by the realities encountered *after* graduation.[7] It would be more accurate to say that postgraduates are shocked by the disparity between public school prescriptions and what they find in society.[8]

One problem that bears attention is the fact that first year high school students and high school seniors are subject to the same rules and thus the same institutional press.

WHAT IS ADOLESCENCE?

There are two philosophic views of the period known as adolescence, each of which provides a very different setting for schools: adolescence may be conceived as something to be enjoyed in and of itself, or it may be considered as something to be surrendered in anticipation of one's future.[9] The latter view is expressed in the following dialogue. "Why go to school?" "To get good grades." "Why get good grades?" "To get into college." "Why go to college?" "To make more money and get a better job."

The view that adolescence should be surrendered in order to prepare for one's future is supported by a particular conception of education and learning. Learning has to hurt, for without pain there is no education. As one parent expressed it, "When I was a boy we had to write any word we misspelled a hundred times." If the student is comfortable he must not be learning. He must be lazy.

What adults in general and schools in particular have failed to see is that adolescents have their own subculture which is essentially dif-

---

[5]See the author's *Alternative Directions for the Social Studies,* International Textbook Co., Scranton, Pa., 1967, Chapter 1.

[6]Waller, *op. cit.* [2] p. 35.

[7]Waller, *op. cit.* [2] pp. 33-35.

[8]Public school prescriptions are supported by state law in many cases. The following is an example: "Each teacher shall endeavor to impress upon the minds of the pupils the principles of morality, truth, justice, patriotism, and a true comprehension of the rights, duties, and dignity of American citizenship, to teach them to avoid idleness, profanity, and falsehood, and to instruct them in manners and morals and the principles of free government." *Education Code.* Sacramento, California: State of California, 1963, vol. I, p. 356. The myth that hard work necessarily leads to success is tempered early in the post-graduation life of the individual for he learns that it is much easier to climb the ladder of success if your father owns the ladder.

[9]Nordstrom, *op. cit.* [1] p. 56.

ferent from that of adults. On the one hand adolescents have been expected to behave as adults; on the other, many adults have immediately imitated aspects of the adolescent subculture. In the case of the former, parents often force dating and the use of cosmetics on young girls; with the latter, girls had no sooner adopted mod dress than they returned home to find their mothers garbed in the same clothing.

MY TEACHERS DON'T CARE

All too often students feel that their teachers don't care. One student perceptively noted, "We know immediately whether or not our teachers want to be here. Some of them simply don't like teaching." When honest with themselves many teachers would have to agree with the students' analysis of the teaching situation. The teacher who doesn't enjoy teaching is frequently hostile to the students.

Students complain when teachers play favorites and also when they don't get enough individual attention. Parents, who often fail to give individual attention to their two or three children, can't understand why their child's teacher, who has one hundred to one hundred and fifty students, doesn't give individual attention to students.

TEACHER PREJUDICE

White teachers often reveal their racial and ethnic prejudice in subtle ways. For example, in one school the administrator—disciplinarian, although aware of the fact that the Mexican-American student involved spoke English, asked the student in Spanish to bring his books and follow him to the office. In other words, when disciplining the student the more lowly native tongue was used. In another case, a Negro boy was confronted by his teacher after class with the following advice: "You had better behave in here or I'll transfer you to Mr. Smith's class and you know what he thinks of your kind."

TEACHER ALWAYS HAS TO BE NUMBER ONE

Teachers are sometimes aware that they dominate the class so that students have little opportunity to express themselves. Students also complain about the teacher who always sets himself above the students —the teacher who always has to demonstrate that he is smarter than the students. The student who does not play the teacher's game is disciplined in some way by the teacher.

CONCLUSION

Adolescence is a challenging period of time. The student is learning to forge ahead and thus upsets traditional authority relationships to which teachers have adjusted their lives. The result is often a conflict between teachers and students. The following case studies vividly depict such discord.

Case Study Number 7-1

PROBLEM STUDENT FACES TEACHER

A boy from a broken home very seldom brings his book, pencil, and paper to class. He needs a haircut, is untidy in his dress, and has a chip on his shoulder. He has been in trouble in other classes.

As his teacher, what should you do?

Case Study Number 7-2

YOUR REACTION TO ROMANTIC INVOLVEMENT OF ONE OF YOUR STUDENTS

You are a first-year male teacher, fresh out of college, and are teaching a Freshman course. Over a period of weeks you notice that Betty has a crush on you and insists on lingering after class every day and running in to you as you leave school. The situation grows more serious, to the point of embarrassment. Betty constantly offers to help you collect papers, hand out assignments, and run general errands. You begin to sense resentment in the class for what appears to be your "favored" treatment of Betty.

You handle the situation by:

Case Study Number 7-3

YOUR REACTION TO A SITUATION IN WHICH YOUR AUTHORITY AS A TEACHER IS BEING CHALLENGED BY A STUDENT

You are teaching a history class to high school juniors, and your training has been in economics. You find that there is one exceptionally bright student in the class who seems to know more history than you do and uses every opportunity to show his knowledge at your expense. The other students are aware of the fact that this particular student may, in fact, know more than the teacher, and this is beginning to affect your authority in the classroom, for he often answers questions that you cannot. You realize that this one student is causing you endless anxiety.

How will you handle this situation?

Case Study Number 7-4

SARCASTIC STUDENT INTERRUPTS CLASS

You are giving what you consider to be a very important lecture in class one day. A boy who is sitting at the rear of the room is making sarcastic comments which the rest of the class finds very amusing and entertaining. He simply speaks out in class interrupting your lecture whenever he feels like it.

What will you do?

Case Study Number 7-5

STUDENT SWEARS IN CLASS

You are conducting a junior high class. Shortly before class is to be dismissed a once-retained, nice, but very socially, psychologically, and academically immature student uses language identified as swearing by classmates and teacher. All eyes turn toward you.

What are you going to do?

Case Study Number 7-6

STUDENT PASSES NOTES

You are conducting a class and you observe a student passing notes. How would you handle this situation?

Case Study Number 7-7

STUDENT PUSHES YOU AND YOU SLAP HIM

Gene has been a problem child ever since he started school. He is now in your class and his behavior has not changed at all. You have tried in every way to reach him and nothing seems to be working. Finally one day you are at your wit's end as he is disturbing the class with his antics. You take him in the hall to talk to him and he becomes loud and outwardly rude. As you try to restrain him he pushes you and makes a motion as if to hit you. As a reflex, more than anything else, you slap him across the face. You know as soon as you struck him that you were in the wrong.

What do you do?

Case Study Number 7-8

YOUR REACTION TO A DISCIPLINE PROBLEM: A BOY TRIES TO SET FIRE TO ANOTHER STUDENT'S HAIR

You are a woman teacher who is assigned to teach an introductory class. The class is composed of a mixture of students from different grade levels (9th-12th grades). There are students who come from upper middle-class families and those who come from low income families. In glancing at the records and test results of the class you observe that there is a wide range in the learning capacity of the students. It is the second day of class. You are still uncertain of your relationship to them and of their reaction to your method of teaching and to your discipline.

The students are not openly disobedient but tend to "test" you by throwing erasers at one another when your back is turned. One boy who has appeared very quiet and polite up to this time suddenly takes out a lighter, lights it, and holds it near the hair of one of the boys who was throwing erasers.

What will your reaction be?

Case Study Number 7-9

YOUR REACTION TO STUDENT DISHONESTY

You are an art teacher in a rather free classroom situation. From across the room, you notice a student furtively placing an object in an unused drawer in the classroom. At your earliest convenience, a few minutes later, you investigate the drawer and discover that the object is a roll of expensive paper which must have been taken from the supply closet. The student has not noticed your discovery and would most likely deny any connection with the roll of paper.

What would you do?

Case Study Number 7-10

MISBEHAVING STUDENTS AT AN ASSEMBLY

Faculty members are not required to sit with their students at school assemblies. The school does not have an auditorium as yet and assemblies are held in the gymnasium.

The city's symphony orchestra is playing at this assembly. Four or five young men are sitting at the top of the bleachers and deliberately making noise; for example, they are dropping books to the floor from the top of the bleachers.

What will you do?

Case Study Number 7-11

YOUR REACTIONS TO PUBLIC DISPLAY OF AFFECTION ON CAMPUS

You are a junior high school teacher. As you are going to your class after lunch, you see one of your male students kissing his girl friend good-bye in the hall. This action is not allowed by the faculty and student organizations at your school.

What is your reaction?

Case Study Number 7-12

SMOKING ON SCHOOL GROUNDS

You are a teacher in the local high school. Jack Ridley, a sophomore in the school, is generally known as a problem student. The school has rigidly enforced a "no smoking" rule on the school grounds. You excuse yourself at the lunch table and leave your fellow male teachers to enter the men's rest room (used by students and faculty alike). Jack Ridley is in the rest room with a lighted cigarette in his mouth.

How would you respond to his smoking?

Case Study Number 7-13

SMOKING AT AN EXTRA CURRICULAR EVENT NOT HELD AT THE SCHOOL

As a high school teacher you have established monthly seminars to be held in students' homes. Teachers from a nearby university are guest speakers. Approximately fifty students attend each seminar. At the second seminar the representative of one of the cliques in the senior class asks you if it is o.k. for the students to smoke.

How will you respond?

Case Study Number 7-14

A STUDENT ATTENDS A SEMINAR WITH ALCOHOL ON HIS BREATH

As a teacher you have established a seminar which meets monthly at the homes of your students. Shortly after the seminar begins one evening, a student comes to you with the information that another male student has alcohol on his breath.

What would your reaction be?

Case Study Number 7-15

A REPORT OF THE USE OF L. S. D. ON A FIELD TRIP

As a teacher in the high school, you have been asked to go along with a group of students on a field trip to a nearby city. The next morning two students who went on the field trip come into your room and report that two of the other students said they took sugar cubes of L. S. D. before boarding the bus.

What would you do?

Case Study Number 7-16

STUDENTS SEEK ADVICE ON USE OF DRUGS

As a teacher and friend, you have been asked for help by some students who have drugs in their possession. They tell you that they want to quit fooling around with the stuff, and they want to get rid of it without selling it for fear of being caught. They have asked you as a friend to help them in this situation.

What are you going to do?

Case Study Number 7-17

GIRL INDICATES SHE IS PREGNANT

You are a member of a secondary school staff. You are looked upon by your students as a good teacher, a trusted adult, and a friend. You tell your students that you would like to help them with any problems they might have, whether school or otherwise. Some time later a girl student of yours approaches you in hysterics and informs you that she is eight weeks' pregnant. You are the first person she has told and looks to you for advice. She does not want to tell her parents, and she also requests that you keep her secret by remaining silent.

What do you do?

Case Study Number 7-18

STUDENT WANTS GRADE FOR EFFORT

You are a teacher. You have just handed back a paper to your students. One student comes up to you and asks why he didn't do as well as his friend. *He* had worked five hours on his paper.

What do you say to him?

Case Study Number 7-19

GRADING IN REMEDIAL CLASSES

You are a ninth grade English teacher. You have one class which is a low one, almost a remedial level. In this class one student, among others, has been a discipline problem all year and has done very poorly in her classwork. You have given her D's for the first semester and the first half of the second semester, although in a better class she would probably have gotten an F. About the last three or four weeks of school she begins to worry about passing and taking part in graduation. She does become a little less of a discipline problem, and does more of her work than she had been doing. You have told the class that they can do extra book reports, among other things, for extra credit, and the girl turns in four book reports the last four weeks of school. You have in the past graded these fairly leniently, and these are worth B's and C's. When you average her grades they come out to about a C— for the semester.

What grade do you give her? No pluses or minuses can be given for a semester grade.

Case Study Number 7-20

STUDENT IS LATE IN HANDING IN REPORT

You have assigned a book review. All information needed was explained including the due date. Adequate time was allowed. All but one student turned in the report when requested. The remaining report was turned in late.

What would you do?

Case Study Number 7-21

STUDENT WANTS TO TAKE TEST A SECOND TIME

You are a secondary school teacher. After handing back the midterm test, one of your students, who had been doing very well all year, comes up to you with her failing test. She tells you she was very tired the day she took the test because her parents had been fighting all night long. She asks you if she can take the test over.

What will your reaction be?

Case Study Number 7-22

YOUR REACTION TO A STUDENT'S FAILURE TO HAND IN A HOMEWORK ASSIGNMENT

You assign a term paper which counts for one-third of the grade. On the day they are due a student informs you that he lost it on the way to school.

What will your reaction be?

Case Study Number 7-23

A STUDENT CHEATS ON AN EXAM

During an important quiz, you observe a student cheating. It was done through reference to notes. The student does not realize you have spotted him, nor do other students seem to realize what has been happening.

What will you do?

Case Study Number 7-24

REACHING A BRIGHT "UNDER-ACHIEVER"

After several exam periods but before progress reports are due, you learn that one of your low-performance students has an I. Q. of 130.

What will you do?

Case Study Number 7-25

DEALING WITH THE SLOW STUDENT IN A FAST CLASS

You are a secondary school teacher who finds at the beginning of the school year that you have a student in one of your classes who is slower than the rest of the class.

What do you do with this student?

Case Study Number 7-26

STUDENT ASKS YOUR POLITICAL VIEWS

Your class is discussing voting distribution in national elections, as well as occupational voting trends. A student asks (1) your voting tendencies, (2) the voting tendencies of other teachers in the school.

What do you answer (and to what degree)?

Case Study Number 7-27

STUDENT SUPPORTS LENIN'S VIEWS

You have a student who is bright and inquisitive and *frank* in his own opinions. One day you are discussing communism and he comes up with the statement that he thinks that Lenin's view was really pretty good and why is everybody so against it?

What is your reaction?

Case Study Number 7-28

TEACHER AND STUDENTS MUST DECIDE WHEN THE RIGHT TO "FREE SPEECH" IS TRULY A RIGHT

Your eleventh grade social studies class places heavy emphasis on current issues. You want to expose your class to controversial matters in order that they may see the complexities of crucial topics and the necessary obligation of involvement under democracy. The pros and cons of a contemporary political issue are discussed in class. The following day a large portion of students, who had been opposed to our government's official position on the issue, hold a protest demonstration during lunch hour. They are expelled.

What will you do?

Case Study Number 7-29

A BOYCOTT OF THE CAFETERIA

You are a teacher having all twelfth grade students. Students call to your attention the fact that some students have been mistreated by cooks in the cafeteria. The case in point is that students who buy one hot dog for twenty-five cents receive a second one for a dime. Some students pick up the second hot dog for a friend who then does not pay as much for an entire lunch. The cooks, disturbed by this, have taken the second hot dog from students who did not originally go through the cafeteria line and thrown this food in the trash can in front of all of the students.

Students have gone through regular channels (student government to the principal) with their grievance. The principal has spoken to the cooks but nothing has happened as a result of this. Students speak to the principal again but he does not want to put any more pressure on the cooks. Your students ask your opinion as to whether or not there should be a school boycott of the cafeteria.

How will you respond?

Case Study Number 7-30

YOUR RESPONSE TO A STUDENT'S FAILURE TO SALUTE THE FLAG

You lead the flag salute in your class, and one of your students refuses to salute.

What is your response?

Case Study Number 7-31

STUDENT COUNCIL WANTS YOU TO DISAGREE WITH ADMINISTRATION

You have been asked to be an advisor to the student council. Surprising as it seems, students wield some power at your school. During one grueling session on policies, a few of the brightest council members back you into a corner. They ask your opinion on a particular policy which the administration condones, but you individually condemn.

What now?

Case Study Number 7-32

DEALING WITH STUDENTS' RACIAL BIASES

As a teacher of eleventh grade social studies you have just begun a unit on poverty in the United States through the study of American history and contemporary events. You have asked your students if they have any ideas as to why many Blacks live in slum areas. A student responds in the following way: "Niggers are lazy, dirty, and smell. They don't want to work. They just want a hand-out."

How will you respond?

Case Study Number 7-33

STUDENTS CRITICIZE TEACHER WHO IS MINORITY GROUP MEMBER

Miss Jane Saki was employed as a teacher in an all-white suburban school. Miss Saki did not mind the few teachers who tried to ignore her in the meetings or did not speak to her on the streets, but when the students began to refer to her as a dirty Jap or Tokyo Jane, she decided to resign. The principal asked her to reconsider her resignation because she was an excellent teacher and he would like for her to remain on his staff. Several students gave a surprise party for her and carried placards with "We want you to stay, Miss Saki."

What would you do if this was your problem?

Case Study Number 7-34

YOUR REACTION TO THE WHITE STUDENTS' ACCUSATION OF FAVORITISM TOWARD THE FEW BLACK STUDENTS IN THE CLASS

You are a secondary teacher in a class with 5 Black students among the majority of whites. You take such care in not alienating the Blacks and being accused of prejudice that instead you are accused by the white students of pampering the Blacks. Whichever way you move at this point will be risky.

How will you handle the situation?

Case Study Number 7-35

A TEACHER'S DECISION IN HANDLING A STUDENT WITH A LANGUAGE PROBLEM

A seventh grade reading teacher has a class of 80% Mexican-Americans, 10% of whom are bilingual. Three of the four bilingual students speak English because they have been conditioned against using Spanish. One unaffected boy has no qualms about speaking Spanish; in fact, though he speaks English, he often answers the teacher in Spanish because he knows the teacher understands Spanish. The rest of the class is beginning to resent him.

What will the teacher do?

Case Study Number 7-36

IMPROVING CULTURALLY DISADVANTAGED STUDENT CAUGHT SMOKING AT SCHOOL (for Female)

One of the students' problem children is in your English composition class. From the beginning, Dora was considered a potential high school dropout. Her home life had never been conducive to studying or self-advancement and because she is a Negro she has had more than the usual disadvantages of the urban poor whites. However, under your extra-special concern and attention she has begun to make a place for herself in the school. Although she still runs around with kids from her low class area she has gained some status and some sense of worth through her rapidly developing ability to express herself. A beautiful essay on her own dreams and aspirations has just won an award in the school literary magazine.

One day while on hall duty you wander into the girl's rest room. The air is heavy with smoke. You wait outside the rest room for the one girl to come out. To your disappointment that girl is Dora.

Now what do you do?

RESPONSES TO CASES

Case Study Number 7-1

PROBLEM STUDENT FACES TEACHER

1. Send him to get his book and supplies and give a tardy slip.
2. Let him just go back to his locker and get his book and supplies.
3. Send him to the Vice-Principal.
4. Give him a drawer in your class in which to keep his book and supplies.
5. Contact his mother and explain the problem.
6. Give him one more chance and tell him it is the last.
7. Give him an "F."
8. ______________________________

____

Case Study Number 7-2

YOUR REACTION TO ROMANTIC INVOLVEMENT OF ONE OF YOUR STUDENTS

1. Ignoring her offers of help for a few days.
2. Talk to her after class about it.
3. Bring in your wife and one-year-old daughter to class one day and introduce them.
4. Avoid her in the halls and after school.
5. Deliberately rely on another student to help you with errands.
6. ______________________________

____

Case Study Number 7-3

YOUR REACTION TO A SITUATION IN WHICH YOUR AUTHORITY AS A TEACHER IS BEING CHALLENGED BY A STUDENT

1. Try to compete with the student by trying to learn more about the subject so that you can regain your authority in the sense that you can answer all the questions.
2. Recognize your weakness in history but assert your authority over the student by the way in which you handle him in the classroom. Make constructive use of his knowledge.
3. Try to avoid calling on him or allowing him to speak in class.
4. If he is deliberately offensive, speak to him alone letting him know that you welcome his remarks but that you will not tolerate disrespect.

5. Attack the problem as one of student discipline and not as a challenge to your authority, recognizing the fact that oftentimes there might be students who know more than you do but that this should not undermine your position in the classroom.
6. ____

____

____

Case Study Number 7-4

SARCASTIC STUDENT INTERRUPTS CLASS

1. Ignore him and his comments and hope that some of the lecture gets across.
2. Single him out and reprimand him. If he continues, then dismiss him.
3. Try to top his sarcasm and put him in his place.
4. Keep him after school for detention.
5. Try to find out why he seems to be vying for so much attention after taking some sort of disciplinary action.
6. ____

____

____

Case Study Number 7-5

STUDENT SWEARS IN CLASS

1. Ignore the situation, trying to act as if you heard nothing.
2. Verbally "spank" the child for using "dirty" language.
3. Assign to be written 200 times before class the next day—"I must not swear."
4. Send the child with a note to the principal's office for disciplining.
5. Deliver a quick sermon on the evils of swearing.
6. Ask the students for their opinions on this kind of language.
7. Ask the student to repeat what he said in socially acceptable language.
8. Ask to see the child in your room after school, having an idea that he is totally unaware.
9. You assign "swearing" as a topic for "research" for the next class.
10. ____

____

____

Case Study Number 7-6

STUDENT PASSES NOTES

1. You intercept the note and read it aloud to the class, hoping that it doesn't contain a caustic comment about you.
2. You intercept it, correct the spelling and grammar errors, and return it with a reprimand.
3. You intercept it, tear it up and drop it in the wastebasket.
4. You intercept it and do nothing at all—returning it, unread, at the end of the period.
5. You ignore it for now and decide to confront the students involved later.
6. You decide to ignore it completely.
7. ______________________________

____

____

Case Study Number 7-7

STUDENT PUSHES YOU AND YOU SLAP HIM

1. Have the boy go to the rest room, wash up and cool off before returning to the room.
2. Send him to the office and hope things will blow over.
3. Go to the principal, explain what happened, and have him take it from there.
4. Call the parent to a conference after school and handle the problem yourself.
5. Do nothing at all and hope things will be forgotten.
6. ______________________________

____

____

Case Study Number 7-8

YOUR REACTION TO A DISCIPLINE PROBLEM: A BOY TRIES TO SET FIRE TO ANOTHER STUDENT'S HAIR

1. Immediately confront the boy in front of the class and confiscate the lighter.
2. Call the boy in after class to discuss the incident to find out why he tried to set fire to the other boy's hair.

3. Say nothing in class but send a note to the counselor relating the incident and referring the boy for guidance and counseling.
4. Dismiss the incident as a practical joke since the boy didn't really set fire to the other boy's hair.

6. ____

____

Case Study Number 7-9

YOUR REACTION TO STUDENT DISHONESTY

1. Call the class' attention to the "misplaced" supplies and give an appropriate lecture to the class as a whole.
2. Confront the student with the evidence and punish him regardless of his denials.
3. Put the paper back in the supply closet, without any other reaction.
4. Leave the paper where the student put it and wait for him to remove it.

5. ____

____

Case Study Number 7-10

MISBEHAVING STUDENTS AT AN ASSEMBLY

1. Ignore the students and hope the assembly will soon end.
2. Ignore the students for the moment and then confront them after the assembly is finished.
3. Move over to the students, tell them to stop the noise, but carry the matter no further.
4. Move over to the students, tell them to stop the noise and report to the principal's office at the end of the assembly.
5. Send the students directly to the principal's office although the assembly is not over.
6. Tell the students you will have their grades lowered for their actions.

7. ____

____

Case Study Number 7-11

YOUR REACTIONS TO PUBLIC DISPLAY OF AFFECTION ON CAMPUS

1. You ignore the incident.
2. You talk to the student after class.

3. You report the incident to the faculty member in charge of the student organization concerned with rule infractions.
4. You punish the boy in your classroom.
5. You inform the girl's teacher.
6. ____

____

Case Study Number 7-12

SMOKING ON SCHOOL GROUNDS

1. Tell Jack that he knows better than to smoke in the rest room, he would be suspended from school if caught, don't do it again, and leave the rest room without reporting the incident to anyone in the school.
2. Act as if you don't see Jack smoking and leave the rest room without comment.
3. Make contact with Jack's parents and see if you can work out this matter jointly.
4. Recommend that Jack be sent to the student court.
5. Send Jack to the principal.
6. Work with the school counselor to help Jack deal with his anti-school behavior.
7. Physically back Jack against the rest room wall hoping that he will be scared and respect your authority.
8. ____

____

Case Study Number 7-13

SMOKING AT AN EXTRA CURRICULAR EVENT NOT HELD AT THE SCHOOL

1. Inform the representative that students their age should not smoke—especially at a function in any way connected with the high school.
2. Inform the representative that seniors in high school are old enough to make their own decisions with regard to this matter.
3. Ask the representative to have his friends not smoke that evening but add that the matter will be taken up in class the following day.
4. Ask the representative to have his friends not smoke that evening but add that the matter will be taken up with some of the individuals involved the following day.
5. Inform the representative that whether or not they should be allowed to smoke is the decision of the host and hostess in the home where the seminar is being held.

6. Ask the representative to pass the word on that they should not smoke that evening but the matter will be dealt with the following day. On the following day, discuss the matter with the high school principal.
7. ______________________________

____

____

Case Study Number 7-14

A STUDENT ATTENDS A SEMINAR WITH ALCOHOL ON HIS BREATH

1. Overlook the situation unless the student with alcohol on his breath becomes obnoxious.
2. Ask the student with alcohol on his breath to leave the seminar.
3. Talk to the student with alcohol on his breath the next day and ask him not to attend future seminars in this state.
4. Discuss the matter in general terms (without reference to the individual involved) the next day in class.
5. Talk to the student with alcohol on his breath later on during the seminar and tell him that he knows better than to come to this group with alcohol on his breath. Do not, however, ask him to leave.
6. ______________________________

____

____

Case Study Number 7-15

A REPORT OF THE USE OF L. S. D. ON A FIELD TRIP

1. Tell the two students who came into your room that you are concerned and then drop the matter without notifying anyone.
2. Take the matter to the principal with the recommendation that the two students who said they took L.S.D. be suspended from school so they cannot brag about their venture to other students.
3. Take the matter to the principal with no recommendation.
4. Talk to other teachers to see what they would do.
5. Call to your room the students who said they took the L.S.D. and get more information before acting.
6. Send the two students who said they took L.S.D. to the principal, ask them to tell the principal what they were doing on the bus, and then meet with the principal to discuss the matter.

7. Take the matter to the next teachers' meeting for group opinion.
8. Notify the local law enforcement officers to check on the students' report.
9. ______________________________

____

____

Case Study Number 7-16

STUDENTS SEEK ADVICE ON USE OF DRUGS

1. Avoid involvement and tell them to work it out among themselves.
2. Report the matter to the police.
3. Tell the students you'll help them as best you can, and then start a campaign against drugs.
4. Say you're sorry, but this could cost you your job—thus they should give themselves up to the police.
5. ______________________________

____

Case Study Number 7-17

GIRL INDICATES SHE IS PREGNANT

1. Tell her she will have to inform her parents because they will find out eventually.
2. Give her the name and address of a doctor for an abortion.
3. Send her to the nurse.
4. Send her to the office.
5. Put her in her parents' position so that she will realize that they are a valuable source of counsel and will therefore go to them with her problem.
6. Tell her to find the father and get married.
7. ______________________________

____

Case Study Number 7-18

STUDENT WANTS GRADE FOR EFFORT

1. You try to explain that it is not the amount of time you put into a paper but the quality of the paper.

2. You suggest that you will re-read it.
3. You allow him to look at someone else's paper so that he can see what constitutes a better paper.
4. ____________________

____

Case Study Number 7-19

GRADING IN REMEDIAL CLASSES

1. Give the student a C.
2. Give the student a D.
3. ____________________

____

Case Study Number 7-20

STUDENT IS LATE IN HANDING IN REPORT

1. Accept the review as turned in and grade it in the same manner as the other reviews.
2. Accept the review but lower the grade.
3. Accept the review but warn of lower grades if tardiness continues.
4. Try to find out by analyzing the report if:
   a. The tardiness involves laziness or extra effort.
   b. Habitual tardiness in papers and poor attendance is involved.
   c. The student realizes that business (society) may not find tardiness acceptable.
5. ____________________

____

Case Study Number 7-21

STUDENT WANTS TO TAKE TEST A SECOND TIME

1. Give her a make-up test.
2. Tell her you won't count the test heavily on her final grade.
3. Tell her you are sorry but if you did this for her other students would hear about it and also come to you with other excuses for doing badly.
4. Call up the girl's parents to see if she was telling the truth.
5. ____________________

____

Case Study Number 7-22

YOUR REACTION TO A STUDENT'S FAILURE TO HAND IN A HOMEWORK ASSIGNMENT

1. Inform him that it's just too bad, but that he'll have to face the consequences—an F if not in; a reduced grade if late.
2. Tell him not to worry. After all he did the work, so you'll just base his grade on the other two-thirds.
3. Tell him to bring in a list of all his references, early drafts, and related materials as proof that he isn't just telling a story.
4. Ask him what grade does he think he would have gotten and then give him that grade.
5. Phone his parents and talk to them about the matter.
6. Give him more time without reducing his grade.
7. Give him a reduced assignment in place of it.
8. ____

   ____

Case Study Number 7-23

A STUDENT CHEATS ON AN EXAM

1. Ignore that you even saw it.
2. Mention it to the student quietly on the side.
3. Mention it to the student on the side and punish him.
4. Take his paper on the spot and make it an open example.
5. ____

   ____

Case Study Number 7-24

REACHING A BRIGHT "UNDER-ACHIEVER"

1. Discuss this problem with a counselor.
2. Reevaluate your teaching techniques.
3. Ask the student probing questions in regard to his home situation.
4. Call the parents and request a conference.
5. Talk to the student individually and allow him to do extra research in an area that interests him.
6. Talk to other teachers about the problem.
7. Talk to the principal.
8. ____

   ____

Case Study Number 7-25

DEALING WITH THE SLOW STUDENT IN A FAST CLASS

1. Slow the class down to his speed.
2. Give him special instruction after school to try to bring him up to the level of the rest of the class, and keep him there.
3. Ignore the problem and hope that he will catch up by himself.
4. Request that he be transferred out of your class into a slower one.
5. ______________________________

____

Case Study Number 7-26

STUDENT ASKS YOUR POLITICAL VIEWS

1. Your opinion, but not those of other teachers.
2. Answer all truthfully.
3. Generalize to "most teachers."
4. ______________________________

____

Case Study Number 7-27

STUDENT SUPPORTS LENIN'S VIEWS

1. Tell him Lenin's thesis is not followed by the communists of today and that they have warped it to the point of making many people fear it for its destructive rather than constructive policies.
2. Tell him about xenophobia and the implications of painting black and white pictures. That he is partially right—and hope he doesn't tell the school board.
3. Ask him to do a report on Lenin's communism vs. Stalin's vs. present day and show the differences.
4. Compare it with different forms of communism (Socialism) in use today. Turn it into a history lesson.
5. ______________________________

____

Case Study Number 7-28

TEACHER AND STUDENTS MUST DECIDE WHEN THE RIGHT TO "FREE SPEECH" IS TRULY A RIGHT

1. Defend the students and their right to free speech and assembly.
2. Remain detached to avoid involvement.

3. Explain to the students that discretion is the better part of valor and that there is a time to remain silent.
4. Persuade the principal that the significance of the issues necessitates further discussion and that an open discussion be held to involve all interested students.
5. ______________________________

____

____

Case Study Number 7-29

A BOYCOTT OF THE CAFETERIA

1. Tell your students that they are well within their rights in a democracy to have a boycott of the cafeteria.
2. Personally lead the boycott and try to master support among students and faculty.
3. Have your students study the use of boycotts in past history but do not commit yourself on this in an overt way.
4. Discourage your students from boycotting the cafeteria in any way possible.
5. Tell your students that they have no right to boycott and such activities have no place in public schools.
6. ______________________________

____

____

Case Study Number 7-30

YOUR RESPONSE TO A STUDENT'S FAILURE TO SALUTE THE FLAG

1. Tell him to salute.
2. Ignore him.
3. Ask him in private why he does not salute.
4. Have a class discussion on the meaning of the flag salute.
5. Send him to the principal for discipline.
6. Make him write an essay on patriotism and the flag salute.
7. Discuss with the class (and the principal) ways to make this patriotic observance more meaningful.
8. ______________________________

____

Case Study Number 7-31

STUDENT COUNCIL WANTS YOU TO DISAGREE WITH ADMINISTRATION

1. You answer the council with the usual pat administrative response.
2. You give the students your own opinion and explain how it differs from that of the administration.
3. You give the council your point of view alone.
4. You hedge and throw the matter back to the council at large, hoping that they will uphold the policy as it stands.
5. You ignore the issue and ask that the topic be dropped—plead the 5th!
6. ____

____

Case Study Number 7-32

DEALING WITH STUDENTS' RACIAL BIASES

1. Immediately challenge the student for using the term "nigger" instead of Black. Then proceed with an analysis of what he said.
2. Overlook the use of the term "nigger" and proceed with an analysis of what the student said.
3. Do not deal with the student's response but instead go on with other questions to the class.
4. Ask the class to respond to the student's comments before you enter the conversation with your ideas.
5. Take the student on with a teacher-student debate in front of the class and then ask for other students' responses.
6. Since you want to be honest with your students, tell the student exactly what you *feel* about his comments even if it means that you become very emotional in front of the class.
7. Set up a special study of Black history in order to change the students' attitudes toward Blacks.
8. Take the class on a field trip to meet Blacks who have become successful.
9. Take the class to a slum area where many Blacks live.
10. ____

____

Case Study Number 7-33

STUDENTS CRITICIZE TEACHER WHO IS MINORITY GROUP MEMBER

1. Forget the students' remarks and remain.
2. Take a chance that the following year might prove better relations.

3. Think about the pay and forget about the people.
4. Thank them for their late kindness, and accept another position in a better community.

5. ______________________________

____

____

Case Study Number 7-34

YOUR REACTION TO THE WHITE STUDENTS' ACCUSATION OF FAVORITISM TOWARD THE FEW BLACK STUDENTS IN THE CLASS

1. Deny the white students' accusation and quietly try to treat both groups equally.
2. Admit that perhaps you were being more lenient with the Black students for fear of being labeled as prejudiced. You explain your situation to the students and say that you will try to resolve it.
3. Deny the white students' accusation, but continue to treat the Black students with special consideration since you feel they might fail if you graded them equally.
4. Admit that you are treating them differently, but you try to convince the white students that they must recognize the need for this differential treatment.

5. ______________________________

____

Case Study Number 7-35

A TEACHER'S DECISION IN HANDLING A STUDENT WITH A LANGUAGE PROBLEM

1. Explain to the boy that his ability to speak Spanish is an advantage and that if he spoke English as well as Spanish, he might be able to get a better job later on. The best way to do this would be to try to keep his mind thinking in English and thus his words English.
2. Let the boy speak some Spanish and, soliciting the help of the other Spanish students, let the class do a unit on the Mexican Culture.
3. Arrange a conference with the parents to find out how badly they want the boy to learn English and base the solution on what they feel.

4. ______________________________

____

Case Study Number 7-36

IMPROVING CULTURALLY DISADVANTAGED STUDENT CAUGHT SMOKING AT SCHOOL (for Female)

1. Assume that some other girls were in there smoking earlier and that Dora really had nothing to do with it. You really have no proof and by pushing the point you may only destroy the constructive relationship that you have developed with her—and may even alienate her from school activities at which she has so recently become adept and interested.
2. Take the risk of expulsion and report her to the principal.
3. Reprimand yourself for ever walking into the girls' rest room in the first place as there is a staff rest room provided for faculty members and it was just by chance that you walked into the rest room used by the students. Cross the incident off as an unfair discovery on your part.
4. Take the girl aside and talk to her yourself—tell her you will let this go and that you don't want to know whether she did it or not, but that she should realize what kind of a position she could put herself in.
5. Go to the principal in private and have him call in the girl to comment on her contribution and emergence in school and the type of conduct she should maintain to retain her new position. This would avoid direct accusation and also the possible severance of your relationship.
6. In conference with the parents of the girl attempt to enlist their help in enforcing school standards. By not calling the girl on the carpet in front of the whole school you might be salvaging the social and personal advancement the girl has made since her start in high school.
7. ______________________________

____

____